Dear Patricia

You absolutely rock!

Thank you for your
huge heart and
for sharing all of who you
are with the world!
Keep on following your
own heart no
matter what!

♡ Shivani

DISCOVER YOUR DHARMA

10 Secrets to Redefine Your Life Purpose through Effective Journaling

SHIVANI SINGH

AVISHA PRESS

The offer on page 148 is open to all purchasers of *Discover Your Dharma* by Shivani Singh. Original proof of purchase is required. The offer is limited to the Discover Your Dharma Intensive Seminar only, and your registration in the seminar is subject to availability and/or changes to program schedule. The course must be completed by December 31, 2010. The value of this 'Two-for-One-Special' is $499.00 as of October 31, 2009, applied only when you and a companion register concurrently. Corporate or organizational purchasers may not use one book to invite more than two people. While participants will be responsible for their travel and other costs, admission to the program is free. Participants in the seminars are under no additional financial obligation whatsoever to Dharma Express, LLC or Shivani Singh. Dharma Express, LLC reserves the right to refuse admission to anyone it believes may disrupt the seminar, and to remove from the premises anyone it believes is disrupting the seminar.

This book is not intended to provide personalized financial, career, medical, psychological, spiritual, or therapeutic advice. Readers are encouraged to seek the counsel of competent professionals with regard to such matters, especially chronic depression, mental, psychological, and emotional instability, financial planning, and career planning. The Author and Publisher specifically disclaim any liability, loss, or risk which is incurred as a consequence, directly or indirectly, of the use and application of any of the contents of this work.

Avisha Press books may be purchased for educational, well-being, or sales promotional use. For information, please write: Group Marketing Department, Avisha Press, 7040 Avenida Encinas, Suite 182, Carlsbad, CA 92011.

FIRST EDITION

Library of Congress Cataloging-in-Pulication Data
Singh, Shivani
Discover your dharma: 10 secrets to redefine your life purpose through effective jour naling/ Shivani Singh
ISBN 978-0-578-03121-7
Library of Congress Control Number: 2009907413

I dedicate this book to
my most beautiful and amazing mother, Radha.
Through your unconditional love and wisdom,
you showed me how to follow
my heart's dharma.

Live each present moment completely
and the future will take care of itself.
Fully enjoy the wonder and
beauty of each instant.

You are the master
of the moments
of your life.

PARAMAHANSA YOGANANDA

ACKNOWLEDGEMENTS

I am honored to have been chosen to author this book. However, no great work can be done alone. To my Guru, Paramahansa Yogananda, I thank you for your blessing in manifesting this book.

To my inspiring mother, Radha, thank you for your ever-constant support, insight, and positive energy every step of the way. Your time, input, ideas, feedback, and unwavering commitment has seen me through the past four years of brainstorming, writing, editing, and revising this book. Without you, this book would not have been possible! To my father, Robby, thank you for encouraging me to pursue my dreams, to follow my heart, and to strive for the Highest! To my dearest sister Nirvana, thank you for believing in me and in the power of this book. Your encouraging words and music helped me to keep on keeping on! To my awesome brother Dhruva, thank you for being a visionary, for seeing the best in me, and for your down-to-earth advice! You are the best family I could ever ask for, and this book is a tribute to your infinite patience and love.

From concept to manifestation, there are a few people I would like to extend my heartfelt gratitude for having a pivotal role in the evolution of this book. To my mentors, Milton Drepaul, T. Harv Eker, Joel and Heidi Roberts – you are indeed diggers of divine deposits. Thank you for your friendship and invaluable wisdom! My dear friends Albert Lin, Irene Chen, Melanie Zauscher, Devon Hughes, Pallavi Vyas, Derek Lomas, Garrett Smith, Nicole Truitt, Srinivas Sukumar, Sujata R. Emani, and Marco Faggella, you never waver from rediscovering your dharma and pursuing your passion! You inspire me, and thank you all for encouraging me to finish this book no matter what, and to be the best that I can be! My divine friends in the Self-Realization Fellowship Monastic Order – thank you for your inspiration, encouragement, feedback, and genuine interest in the spirit of this book. To Prof. John Roads, thank you posthumously, for believing in my potential, and the success of this endeavor; your unstoppable spirit will always remind me to live life with zest. Thank you also to those friends in the future who will be vital to the support, awareness, and distribution of this work.

I am grateful to all of my friends and family around the world who have held this vision and whose unwavering faith in me have made this book a reality.

More than anything else, I am grateful to you, my reader, for having the courage to open this book, and to give yourself permission to discover your dharma through the magic of journaling.

DHARMA

{definition}

n. One's essential duty; right action; one's higher purpose in life.

The highest dharma is to recognize the Truth in one's own heart, to fully realize one's True Self.

Salutation of the Dawn

Listen, to the exhortation of the Dawn!

Look to this Day
For it is life, the very Life of life!
In its brief course
Lie all the verities and realities of your existence:

The bliss of growth
The glory of action
The splendour of beauty

For Yesterday is but a Dream
And Tomorrow only a Vision
But Today well lived makes every Yesterday
a Dream of Happiness
And every Tomorrow a Vision of Hope.

Look well, therefore to this Day!
Such is the Salutation of the Dawn.

K A L I D A S A

Indian Sanskrit Poet, 4th Century, A.D.

CONTENTS

FOREWORD

Using the Timeless Secrets in *Discover Your Dharma*, The Imminent Explorer Defied the Unnatural Urge to Become A Mid-Level Drone

From the beginning of consciousness we are hunted by the question of our own purpose - 'Why am I here and what is my destiny?' Through a systematic study of history's most inspiring individuals, Shivani Singh has uncovered ten secrets of discovering the answers to that lifelong quest we all share. In this valuable book, Shivani shares a practical approach to cast away the fog of confusion and enable our own active participation in the acquisition of our destiny. The following pages have the ability to permanently change your life, if you are ready and willing to commit yourself with an open ear to the voice that exists within you.

Several years ago, I found myself within the midst of a bewildering quarter-life crisis. Entangled in a career path I was not sure I wanted, reeling from the emotional war of a messy breakup, and lost in the void of a dangerously passionate existential reflection, I was in graduate school. Losing myself in piles of numbers, equations, papers, and expectations, I had grown a dread for the nagging sense of disappointment in the life I was headed for. How was I going to change the world when I was stuck in a degree that would inevitably funnel me into a midlevel position at some engineering supergiant corporation, forcing me into a life of security and boredom? This could not be my fate. I wasn't another drone. I was special! *I was destined for greatness...* at least, that was what I had thought. But I, like many others, had stopped listening to that inner confidence. I was choosing more and more to play the game society had so unscrupulously set up for us. Worst of all, I was beginning to think there were no other options.

On one special day, the voice of a young woman named Shivani Singh, came trailing in through the door of the tiny office that I shared with two other equally miserable graduate students. Though muffled through the thick wooden door of the adjacent office, her confidence and enthusiasm transmitted the presence of a kindred spirit. Moments later my advisor, whom I endearingly called "El Capitan," dashed into the room brandishing a beautiful smiling girl.

"Albert!" he proclaimed. "This is the new star of the materials science department! She worked with NASA, she's writing a book about the meaning of life, and she's got it all figured out. Talk to her so you can stop being so depressed!"

And talk we did. We talked for hours, weeks, then years about our dreams, our passions, and this thing we eventually called our "Dharma." We inspired each other in the way friends should, encouraging ourselves to cast aside the doubt of all the "naysayers" and simply believe that the world was truly our oyster. We toiled over the choices of careers, and discussed the reasons in which these decisions were so difficult. The more we discussed, the more we realized that the decision was not the difficult part. The difficult part was choosing whether to believe in our dreams or to believe in the square-box identities the world had placed upon us. This choice is clear within the sanguinity of hindsight. Yet, while bogged down in the throes of expectations and pressure, it was difficult to identify with a dream that is often dismissed as "childish," rather than noble and attainable.

Now, over three years since Shivani came in through that office door, I find myself well on a path towards the realization of my own amazing dharma. While reading the words in the following chapters, I realized that Shivani had not only found a way to believe in herself, but had been helping me see my own dreams as important too. She had found a system in the madness of figuring out what we were meant to do with our lives, and this is what she shares with us in this book.

In this age of chaotic "progress," it has become easy to replace our true dreams with the seemingly more attainable metrics of societal successes. We find ourselves entrenched in identities that we had never really intended on adopting, but are undeniably afraid of leaving. We surround ourselves with distractions and noise to hide the fact that we are wasting our one chance to live the life we want, so much so that the pain that accompanies the glimpses of clarity are unbearable and we would rather continue distracting ourselves than confront our own lack of action.

This is your chance to change that, to face your void of true fulfillment, and replace it with a clear vision of your internal Dharma. This book will not tell you what that Dharma is, for no external source can. Rather, it will provide you the mechanisms towards realizing the answers to your highest calling that have been there all along.

Dr. Albert Yu-Min Lin
P.I. of Valley of the Khans Project
Research Scientist & Explorer,
University of California, San Diego
La Jolla, California, May 29th, 2009

THE SHIVANI STORY

How the Young Rocket Scientist Discovered the Secrets to Finding Her Dharma

I had always dreamed of working at NASA. By the time I was 17 years old, I had landed a position as a young physics researcher on one of NASA's spacecraft missions. Working alongside some of the world's greatest geniuses and engineers at JPL, Boeing, and NASA, I was over the moon with excitement. It felt like a dream come true. I soon grew in experience and responsibility – often working until late in the lab, working extra hours on the weekends, and business as usual during summer, winter, and spring breaks. After three years, the not-so-glamorous research life soon took its toll. Somewhere between the inevitable budget cuts and uncompromising projects, long meetings and time-consuming grant proposals, the passion for astrophysics I had started out with had become flattened under stacks of merciless paperwork. I, the unstoppable superstar scientist with amazing potential, had become a frenetic, disillusioned, downtrodden, invisible robot… going day in and day out, with out any end in sight!

As August rolled into December, I dreaded another long winter break in the lab. I felt I couldn't go in one more day. I didn't want to trade my happiness for success any more. I wanted both!

I spent a lot of nights bummed out at myself – *what am I doing here? Why am I doing this? What to do next?* I felt there was no way out, that nobody understood that haunting discontentment that hung in my heart. I felt utterly lost, confused, and clueless. Alone. Purposeless. Like a loser, who should quit complaining, suck it up, and do what people in the real world do – work in the best job you could get, and then stay for the long haul. I would often get my colleague's unsympathetic response:

Why would you leave your dream job?
You're good at what you do - you should stay and stick it out!
Rewards come way later in life – everybody feels like you.
Life isn't perfect. Deal with it!

Even though I sort of agreed with them, the truth was I wasn't just looking for another job or a career change. I was after that *something* else that would make my life meaningful, that would make a difference in mankind, and that would rock my world.

What direction should I take now? Instead of heading to the moon, I headed to… India. Known as the ancient land of wisdom and spirituality, I hoped India would be a place I would discover my dharma - that higher purpose to why I am on this planet, and the work I must do. Leaving behind sunny San Diego for an exotic land I had only read about, I didn't know when I would come back to the United States. I was ready for some major soul-searching, a much needed spiritual journey to find the answers to those questions that haunted me at night. With a bursting heart, I traveled to many ashrams, meditated under banyan trees, chanted for nights on end, and went to the holiest places. I had the privilege of serving food to leper colonies, and spending time in seclusion in the Himalayas. Week after week, I visited temples, schools, slums, and bathing ghats, from Calcutta to Varanasi, and Uttar Pradesh to Allahabad.

Traveling a total of 240 hours by train, I often looked forward to these times to journal. With experiences fresh in my mind, I would rush to capture the moment with my pen. Flooding the pages with images and emotions, my journal became more than a book to record events. My head reeling from the overwhelming sights, sounds, and smells that inundated me, I would be forced to process the intensity of my experiences through my trusty journal. On the longer train rides, I would write for hours in my journal, often asking myself questions, writing my experiences, figuring out what they meant for me in the moment, and observing my growth from day to day. I learned a lot about what tugged at my heart strings, and what I wanted most out of life... I wanted to give, to share, to open, and to empower. I just didn't know how – yet!

With all the traveling and serving, meditating, and questioning, the answers weren't to be found by looking on the outside. They could only be found by looking *inside*. While I didn't quite know how to go about finding the answers on the inside, I knew I didn't need to be in India to do it. And so, I finally returned home to sunny Southern California.

It took me a couple of weeks to get adjusted to life back in the U.S. It seemed the million-dollar question everyone asked was, 'So.... What's next?' It was often painful. I wanted so much to know what to do next, but I felt so confused. I thought back to my travels in India – where the days were so full, where I felt so alive, and where everything was imperfectly perfect, in its own chaotic way. If only I could live so fully in the moment here! I wished I could somehow extract the essence of those experiences again, and recreate them in my life. I reached for my journals in my dusty backpack, and sitting at my kitchen table in the pale afternoon light, I began to experience a new dimension of my journey.

As I read through those weathered beaten-up journals, I started realizing that journaling is not just for introspection, therapy, or a diary of events. Journaling was actually much more powerful as an experiential process. I looked at where my consciousness was at the beginning of the trip – superficial expectations of a girl who had just graduated from a top university, coming from the U.S, looking to roam around India and mystically discover my special life mission that I was born to do. After two months of journaling, it had become a tool to hear my own voice when I felt I had none, a process of acquiring answers that I could find nowhere else, and a means of finding a peace, an understanding, a renewal of spirit, and an ever-new treasure chest of power I never knew I had.

That was when I had my Aha! Moment.

If the process and power of journaling could work in the middle of Calcutta's Howrah train station as I waited 8 hours for the next train, amidst the incessant bell ringing, music blaring, and thousands of bustling travelers coming and going, it could work anywhere!

Moved by necessity, under the extremest of conditions, I had unwittingly used journaling to find the answers to my dharma. From writing super duper fast before the train left, to writing down all that I was truly grateful for at night, I started to see the techniques and trends that had emerged in my journaling, with amazing results.

Being the scientist I was, I had a strong affinity for systems and formulas. In order for things to be repeated – there must be an easy process to follow with consistent results. Recreating the conditions, I saw that there were 'templates' that I followed, with stunning success. I could do it right here in my home, and find answers to everyday questions – about relationships, fears, what to do next, and why. To substantiate my finding, I decided to embark on a rigorous research pursuit. There must have been other people who were movers and shakers, who knew and practiced these secrets, too. I started with people I admired and wanted to emulate. People like Gandhi, Mother Teresa, Leonardo Da Vinci, and Walt Disney. I started with people who inspired me – from Pablo Picasso to John F. Kennedy, and Anne Frank to Henry David Thoreau. Each of them had to make many tough decisions to follow their hearts against all voices of reason around them. And each of them practiced their predominant 'dharma secret' with fervor. More importantly, they were a success – in their own eyes, and eventually, the eyes of the world. They lived by their rules, and pursued their dharma, even when it seemed crazy, or difficult, or impossible. They were passionate, purposeful, and serviceful to others in their own way. And they became larger than life.

I created this system of 10 Secrets so that anybody, with any background, any belief system, from any walk of life, could do these techniques, and attain notable results. I started to share the process with others at workshops, universities, hospitals, retreats, get-togethers, meetings, conferences, and online. Soon, I began to get amazing feedback from people all over the world – Germany, Australia, India, Japan, Brazil, Paris, London, Vancouver, Suriname, Trinidad, and all over the US – New York, Miami, Washington D.C., Seattle, Chicago, Massachusetts, Texas, Oregon, Nevada, Virginia, and all over California – from San Francisco to San Diego. I was thrilled to hear from colleagues, engineers, financial advisors, yoga teachers, therapists, chiropractors, monks, teachers, professors, parents, college students, working professionals, and entrepreneurs, who all used these techniques with stunning, tangible success.

As we usher in a new era of 'Yes, We Can!' we are called to step up to the plate, to stop playing small, to stand in our own power, and follow our dharma. We don't have time to waste trying this and that before we know our dharma. We want to be passionate and on purpose NOW!

I urge you to ask yourself: What if this could really be an easier way to know why we are here and what we must do next? What if we tried this new way, and it worked? What if we taught this to our children, and our children's children? What would the world look like then? What if in the next generation, we had less mid-life and quarter-life crisis, and more contentment earlier in life? What if we had less bitterness and regret, and lived lives more authentically, more consciously, and more joyously? What if we knew at 21 or 31 what most people figure out at 51 or 81 about the true treasures of life? That instead of just 'getting-by' in a mediocre life, we could in fact, wherever we are, have that glorious dharma we were born to live, NOW? Do YOU want to be one of those people?

YES?

Then turn the page and get moving!

A UNIQUE INTRODUCTION

For the Savvy and Sophisticated Dharma Seeker

Of all the wondrous discoveries you have ever made, none can compare to the greatest and most glorious discovery of all - Your Dharma. There is no mission more magnificent, no duty more daunting, and no desire more compelling, than the longing to know: who you truly are, that you are loved beyond measure, and that there is a purpose to your existence.

For millennia, we mistakenly equated our true selves with our jobs, our bank accounts, our relationships, and our accomplishments (or lack thereof), because these were the metrics society measured us by. People loved us or dismissed us based on our relationship status, our job title, our looks, and how much we earned. Since we wanted to be happy, worthy, and loved, we were constantly after that grand life purpose which would give us those outer things. Until we find that grand life purpose, we are frustrated, depressed, and outcasted somehow – from ourselves, our family, and our society. It seems that no matter what we do, there is always that nagging sense of discontentment that follows us wherever we go, until we actually take action and do something about it.

We have been sold the idea that if we are discontented, it means that we are off track. We think that we made a bad choice, and that is why we suffer with a sense of uneasiness that plagues our souls. If we had made a better choice, we would be contented, and we would have no reason to question why we are here or what we must do next. In this state of discontentment, we have a tendency to think that we 'missed out;' that if we had only done things differently, we would be happier right now. What we fail to realize is that discontentment is a normal part of our human existence. Just like hunger is a sign that we need to eat our next meal, discontentment is a sign that we are ready for what is 'next' for us in life. Whether it is a new relationship or a new job, a new perspective or a new way of being, discontentment is what prods us along in our own evolution. Without discontentment, we would have no cause to seek new experiences, new thoughts or ideas, new people, or new ways of doing and being. If we were forever contented with where we are, we would never have any reason to change or grow.

In this book you will find the Secrets to overcoming that nagging sense of discontentment that plagues your soul. Life is ever new, ever-changing, and ever dynamic. What you may think is your life purpose today, can be out the window tomorrow. There is no security in the traditional definition of a 'life calling' or 'life purpose.' Maybe you were meant to be an Olympic gymnast – that's your passion in life. But what if you got in a car accident and became paralyzed? Does that mean your life purpose is over? No! If this so-called grandiose life purpose can be shattered in an instant, why are you still seeking it out? There's got to be something more to life than a 'role' you have to stick with for all eternity!

Through a systematic, concrete, and powerful process, this book reveals the Secrets to *know* your dharma - what is the right action to take *now.* As your circumstances, relationships, passions, abilities, and consciousness change from day to day, these moments of discontentment will arise to prod you along in your evolution. Unfortunately, it is not always clear what to do next if you do not have the right tools to help you. Luckily for you, all the tools you need in order to decipher what your heart is telling you, are given in this book.

These 10 Secrets will show you how to Wash Out the Gunk, how to Know your Moment of Truth, and how to Go Beyond the Line. When you feel you are not cut-out for this 'dharma thing,' you will learn how to Shatter the Myths and to Follow Your Heart No Matter What. As you gain clarity on how to feel right about what you do, or do what you feel right about, you will discover how to Be Your Own Visionnaire and Fuel Your Mission with Volition. And in the quiet sanctities of your soul, you will find the transformation you seek as you Do Your Dailies, Stay Connected Within, and Embrace the Gifts of Your Life.

In the process of reading and practicing these 10 Secrets to Discover Your Dharma, you will realize that this is a hybrid of a self-help guide and a workbook in one. While I will hold your hand through the entire process, only you can know what your dharma is for you. Knowing your dharma sometimes means letting go of what other people have told you, expected of you, or want for you. It means discovering, trusting, and owning your voice, your vision, and your capacity to fully realize your Self in every way imaginable.

What this Book will Do for You

Designed for the savvy modern dharma seeker, this book provides a uniquely practical, step-by-step process to enable you on your journey of discovery.

The 30 Minute Rule:

We all have busy lives, and barely have time to get a good night's sleep, much more to spend a lot of time pontificating about life. So I created every Secret in this book to abide by the 30-Minute Rule. Each Dharma Secret takes approximately 10-20 minutes to read, and about 10 minutes to practice on your own for effective results. You can do these Secrets just before going to bed, once a week on Saturday afternoons, or all in one day, if you wish. The point is to learn the principles and the techniques so you can discover your dharma *now*!

Journaling Music for the Dharma Seeker:

This is a unique learning and doing book, complete with customized soundtracks to each technique for your own personal journaling experience. I specifically created and recorded each Soundtrack to help you go deeper and get the most out of your exercise. This journaling music was also intended to be played as you read the book, to open your mind and heart to your dharma that is about to emerge. This isn't ordinary relaxing music. The timing, tones, rhythm, tempo, and melody were especially orchestrated to accompany you as you practice the process outlined in each Secret. Enjoy!

All-in-One Combo:

Each Dharma Secret is applicable in every arena of your Dharma Wheel: your spirituality, your relationships, your recreation, your health and well-being, and your career. This book assumes you are a holistic human being whose dharma involves the interconnection of all aspects of your life, at all times. Whatever is the right thing to do next – from starting your own business to accepting a marriage proposal – these 10 Secrets will help you know the answer to your questions inside.

Left Brain + Right Brain:

The Secrets presented in this book were designed to actively engage both your left *and* right brains. Yes, you want to be passionate and do what you love, but you also want to stay on track, plan ahead, and be conscious of the choices you make. You need both feeling and reason, vision and logic, imagination and concentration, to discover your dharma.

Some Secrets will require your right brained faculties – creativity, insight, intuition, and foresight. Others will require your logic, analysis, introspection, and attention to detail. By the end of this book, you would have enabled all of your faculties to fully realize your unique dharma – not just your favorite hobbies, childhood dreams, or career choices.

High Speed Dharma Access:

In today's hectic world, you don't have time to practice these Secrets for hours before you get benefits. You want answers to your dharma right away! This book targets all three learning styles at once – helping you learn 3 times as fast, and retain information 3 times as long. Involving your audio, visual, and kinesthetic senses, the exercises are structured to help you attain the Secret yourself. All you have to do is pull out your pen and journal, and follow the instructions given in each chapter. After practicing each technique one or two times, you will become a pro. More than that, you will receive the benefits immediately.

Tips to Keep in Mind When Using this Book

Based on the principle that only you can discover your own dharma, the core of this book revolves around doing the experiential exercises given in each of the Secrets in the order they are given. Before we learned how to add numbers, we first learned the principle of addition, we saw an example or two, and then we did addition exercises ourselves. This combination helped us to fully understand the why, how, and when to add numbers, and gave us the ability to add anything for the rest of our lives. When we have mastered addition, we could then learn subtraction. The exact process must be applied when using this book to discover your dharma. The principles, examples, and exercises must be read, understood, and practiced in order to fully attain the Secret. Once that is accomplished, you can proceed to the next Secret. Each Secret builds on the concepts, techniques, and wisdom acquired from the previous Secrets. Therefore, it is imperative to do the techniques as you read them in the book to obtain maximum results.

Discovering and living your dharma requires intuition, creativity, and openness, as well as logic, will power, and right action. This is achieved through the unique format of this book. The following Secrets are presented through a delightful blend of history, art, science, personal stories, modern wisdom, live music, and journaling techniques. Each of these components tap into different parts of your brain, your psyche, approach, and thought processes. As a result, your dharma will unfold in a balanced way, incorporating both feeling and reason, vision and right action.

Dharma Discovery Journaling ToolKit™
Before reading this book, here are a few things you will need in order to effectively discover your dharma:

1. **A pen.**

2. **A BRAND NEW JOURNAL.** You are about to embark on a journey of a lifetime – this journal better be something special! If you got the Dharma Discovery System™ with the guided Journal and *Discover Your Dharma Soundtrack,* then you're all set! For Dharma-Inspired Journals, check out www.dharmaexpress.com for more details!

3. **The *Discover Your Dharma Soundtrack CD*** that is a companion to this book. If you haven't gotten your Soundtrack CD yet, go to www.dharmaexpress.com to purchase and download the CD online. Each of the music tracks were especially created to guide you through the processes given in each Secret.

4. **5-10 minutes.** Whenever you come to this book, create your journaling ambience ~ set aside at least **5 minutes** for yourself, (no checking email, answering your phone etc.,) and light some candles and incense. The idea is to have a short 'ritual' that enables you to relax, reflect, and be open to the transformative experience.

5. **Turn on your music player** (your mobile, iPod™, stereo, or computer) and play the designated music track from the Discover Your Dharma Soundtrack CD

It is my sincerest hope that in this journey of discovering your dharma, you will know that you are loved beyond measure and within you is all that you seek.

In 1903, Einstein discovered the equation that would measure the energy of the universe. In 1965, Watson and Crick unraveled the helix of DNA that would come to be known the world over as the 'stuff life is made of.' And in this moment, you are destined to make the discovery of a lifetime: your dharma.

Embrace the fears, the frustration, the sense of discontentment that haunts you wherever you go. This is your key to discovery, liberation, and enlightenment! Everything you have ever done, all the people you have ever known, and all that you have ever experienced, has fulfilled your dharma until now. There is no such thing as being 'off-track' with your life. It is all part of your life. In fact, it is all a part of you. No more do you have to be someone you are not! No more do you have to hide who you are! No more do you have to stand in the shadows of the past! Step into the Light of Your dazzling brilliance!

You were meant to S T A N D out!

Just go for it –

Discover and Live Your Dharma!

SECRET #1

Wash out the Gunk

There are scriptures and scrolls, wisdom new and old, telling us why we are here, how we should live, and what the purpose of our lives is. Except, we do not want to be told! We want to discover our dharma for ourselves! Call it self-righteous, rebellious, or sacrilegious at the end of the day we are the only ones who have the answers for our lives.

I cannot tell you what to do with your life. Only *you* know what is best for your life. The problem is: how exactly do you *find* those answers for yourself? How do you *know* what is your dharma and the next step for you?

It is an age-old myth that the moment we grow-up (whenever that might be), we will wake up one fine morning, the sun will burst through, and voila! we will see our life purpose, as clear as the blue sky above. It will be so clear we would not have to pontificate about it. *We would just know.* Nothing much to it – it's as easy as pie. Everyone figured out his dharma thus far. When it's our time, we will know too.

Yeah right.

First of all, who do you know has their life purpose figured out? How did they figure it out? And are they willing to show you how they did it? If they were lucky enough to just 'know,' then how long do you have to wait until you get lucky, too?

It seems pretty random, this business of knowing your life purpose, doesn't it? Some people know theirs, while others do not. Yet, *we all have a purpose,* so there must be some way of knowing our calling, right? That is exactly what I thought as I began my own journey to discover the secrets to knowing my my life purpose. From high tech NASA to the solitary foothills of the Himalayas, I sought the key to unlocking that age-old myth that once tortured my soul. As I journeyed throughout India, I found that my life purpose was really my dharma. Dharma is an ever-evolving, dynamic process of taking right action from moment to moment. But, in order to find the right action to take, one must have clarity. Clarity, it turns out, does not come from the sky, but one's own mind. The answers are not to be found on the outside, but the inside, and they are easy to read when the mind is in tune with the heart.

It all comes down to a science, a journaling methodology that you can practice right here, right now, to discover *your* dharma. There really is no other book out there that shows you how exactly to go about discovering your dharma. For the first time, these Dharma Secrets are revealed – what they are, how they work, and how to do them to attain effective results. In perfecting these Secrets, Secret #1 clears the mind so that there is clarity. Secrets #2 through #5 tunes the mind with the heart, and Secrets #6 through #10 teaches us how to read and express that clarity in our lives and in our world.

It often seems that happy, successful people know who they are, what they are about, and where they are going in life. Conversely, we must be miserable failures if we are not clear about where we are going or what we want! That kind of thinking is what holds us back.

The first order of action is to clear the mind.

Without clarity, it is hard to see where we are going, and what we must do next. Have you ever worked on a computer that had so many programs running at once, it froze? Do you ever feel like that, where you have so many options whizzing around in your head, you freeze? According to the great genius Dr. Claude Shannon, the founding father of information theory, this event is called 'information overload.' This occurs when the 'information generators' are generating data faster than the information can be channeled, evaluated, and stored.[1] The quickest way for information to be delivered is to have a clear path to travel. Similarly, the quickest way to know what to do next is to have a clear mind.

Clear your mind to access the answers that are already under the surface, waiting to guide you in your life.

*Imagine a still, stagnant, sluggish river…*a lot of silt and debris, dead branches, and slimy algae sitting in mirk. Everything has piled up over time, and it is more like a stuck pond than a river. Now imagine there is a huge torrential rain pouring down in all its power. With the winds roaring in all directions and the rains pounding incessantly, the water in the river rises and begins to move at a terrific speed, taking everything in its way with the accelerating currents. All of the rocks,

---

[1] Claude E. Shannon. A Mathematical Theory of Communication. *Bell Syst. Tech. J.*, 27:379–423, 623–656, July, October 1948.

grime, and dead branches, are completely flushed out as the rains beat down in torrents and the river rushes at top speed. Soon, the billowing winds calm and the rains lessen into a rhythmic pitter-patter; the river moves with a gentle murmur. After the torrential rains and flood, the river finds its own ebb and flow, the water is clear, and the river is cleansed. It is easy to see where it is going, and you could even see the bottom....fishes, rocks, and the river bed below.

That is what we want to do - wash out the gunk or 'mind babble' that makes us feel 'stuck', and come to a place of clarity, where we feel at ease and in alignment with our inner flow.

The gunk is our fears - those muddy thoughts that go round and round in our heads like a broken record, holding us back from living our lives in the present. That broken record says the same old thing over and over: "Oh, I'll do that when I have the money... when I have the time...when I get a job... when I get married...when the kids go off to college... when I retire..." Sounds familiar? You know the routine. We are experts at telling ourselves that we don't have the time to listen to what is really important: our inner voice. Instead, we talk to friends, check things up on the internet, find a psychic, or run across advice in a magazine column – anything to 'guide' us in the right direction, without having to sit down and introspect on our own.

In a society where the average attention span is pushing 3 minutes, and the mental habit of jumping from task to task every 15 seconds, the gunk is the sum total of all those thoughts that occupy our mind, making petty things extremely important. As soon as we have a moment that we could sit and be with ourselves, we think, "Oh, I have no time for this dharma stuff, I have to call Jen. I have to go to dinner with Peter and Chloe. I wanted to watch this new movie. My favorite TV show is on…" And on and on our mind babbles. Filling our head with gunk. Over time, the gunk piles up, and we cannot see our way any more. It clouds up our perspective, shrouds out our inner voice, and hides our light.

When we have too many choices in front of us, we feel overwhelmed, and can't think straight. If we have been stuck for days, months, or even years, we are experts at making elaborate excuses. These excuses are thoughts that we choose to have in order to be our lesser selves.

We choose to perpetually exist in this state of confusion so we can hide in our own shadows and not be responsible for our own greatness.

If you have the same problem I had, then you know without a doubt that you have amazing potential beyond measure. You feel like you have no idea where to begin, or what to do next. When you consider 'what you want to be,' do you think of just one thing? Probably not! You may want to be an ardent surfer, a multi-million-dollar homeowner, a parent, a world traveler, a freelance writer, a photographer, an academic professor, a dancer, a business owner, *and* an interior decorator. Some of these you might want to do professionally, some you may do just for fun, some you could do at different intensities at different times of your life, and some you can do all at once. The dilemma is: what were you born to do? And how do you know which path to pursue *now*?

In practicing *Secret #1: Wash out the Gunk,* you will have an emergence of everything you want to do now, and you can choose how, when, or whether you want to pursue it at all. You will begin to see your dharma unfolding.

I was not so lucky to find out about this First Secret from a nurturing seminar or an inspiring book. I was just a really frustrated, impatient college student with a lot of questions, feelings, thoughts, and a sense of urgency to have it all figured out NOW! This sense of urgency propelled me to scribble ceaselessly my thoughts, ideas, questions, hopes, desires, and fears. Over the years, this Stream of Consciousness Journaling Technique became a solace to the gnawing hunger for answers and clarity. I often questioned, *what am I supposed to do with my life? Should I stick with what I am doing, or should I do something else?*

My core problem was that I had all these exciting 'paths' to pursue, and I was not sure which one to begin. Do I tackle science research, or travel the world, write books, and give workshops? Maybe I could be a musician and artist, and open my own studio? The list went on and on. The one thing I noticed was that every time I wrote in a frenzy, something magical happened. It was like an inner torrential rain that flooded my mind, washing away the confusion… and all that was left was that quiet clear voice of my intuition.

When you write super duper fast without thinking, your mind can't keep up. You just speed right by to get to what you really want to hear – your inner voice, your true feelings, and your wisdom. From this place, you are better able to sort out all the things you want to undertake, and have a clear idea as to what to pursue NOW.

Are you excited to practice Secret #1?

Secret # 1: Wash out the Gunk
Through Stream of Consciousness Journaling

1. Carefully read the Dharma Discovery ToolKit prep tips in the introduction of this book before practicing this technique.

2. Create your journaling ambience ~ set aside at least **5 minutes** for yourself, (no checking email, answering your phone etc.,) and light some candles and incense.

3. Turn on your music player (like your iPod™, stereo, or computer) and play the first music track, *Wash Your Gunk SoundTrack,* from the Discover Your Dharma Soundtrack Album.

4. Open your journal, and on the first page, write the date, the exact time, and the location:
   Example: 3.7.2009 8:52 PM My room, Boston

5. Take 3 deep breaths...breathe....and relax. Feel the magic of the moment. Close your eyes and feel the torrents of rain beating down and washing out all of the gunk.

6. Now open your eyes, put your pen to paper, and start writing anything... words, feelings, thoughts, ideas... AS FAST AS YOU CAN! Let the rains begin!*
   There are only 2 rules:
   Rule #1: Write at lightning speed!
   Rule #2: Keep writing until the music stops.

7. When the music stops, put your pen down, and close your journal with a BANG! (That's to make sure you know that the gunk is now out of your mind and tucked away safely in your Journal.)

8. Relax and exhale deeply. Feel the breath flowing in and out, like the clear river flowing in its own ebb and flow. Smile! YOU DID IT! You are now ready to discover Your Dharma!

Stream of Consciousness Journal Tip*

Speed is of the essence here. The content and legibility are totally unimportant. Just think of the torrential rains washing out the gunk. The faster you write the more junk you're washing out. Remember, that gunk is covering the wisdom and clarity underneath. Just try it. It works! If it doesn't work, then you just have to write faster without stopping for a longer time. That's all. But it *will* work.

EXAMPLE of Secret #1: Wash out the Gunk

> *Writing super duper fast I don't know what to write writing super duper fast I am sick and tired of everything and everybody… my whole life something is sort of missing… I don't know what it is. Why? Arrgh… this is kinda frustrating I really can't write as fast as my mind is going. In fact I can't remember the last time I used pen and paper! I feel trapped, that my life is passing me by. Why do I have to fight to be happy?I am so tired of going from job to job …*

You get the gist of it? Now, it's time to try it yourself!

Remember, no matter what you write, how you write, or how many pages are whizzing by, write super duper fast and keep your pen going. That's the Stream of Consciousness technique. You can use it at anytime, no matter what is going on in your life. But with these specific prompts, you will get closer to discovering and manifesting your dharma in no time flat. This practice is critical to your success. Follow the technique exactly as it is given in this chapter, and you will see your mind moving from confusion to clarity.

So what are you waiting for? I thought you couldn't wait another second to find out what rocks your world? Grab your pen and paper and let the torrential rain begin!

After Washing out the Gunk, you are now ready for Secret #2, where you will discover your Moment of Truth.

When you hear the splash
Of the water drops that fall
Into the stone bowl,
You will feel that all the dust
Of your mind is washed away.

Sen-No-Rikyu, Zen Tea Master

SECRET #2

Know Your Moment of Truth

Traveling by train on a business trip in South Africa, 24-year old Mohandas Gandhi discovered his dharma en route from Durban to Pretoria, almost overnight. When the train made a stop at 9 p.m. in the city of Maritzberg, a new European passenger boarded Gandhi's first class compartment. The European passenger was shocked to meet an Indian in the first class compartment, and railway officials were called to move the young Indian lawyer to the van compartment.

"But I have a first class ticket," Gandhi protested.

"You must leave this compartment, or else I shall have to call a police constable to push you out." The railway official threatened.

The constable came, grabbed Gandhi's hand, and shoved him out of the train. Gandhi had refused to go to the lower compartment, and the train steamed away without him. The railway authorities took Gandhi's luggage, and locked it up at the train station. Freezing from the brutal mountain air, Gandhi thought of his jacket that was in his luggage as he turned to wait in the waiting room. Lest he be insulted again, Gandhi dared not ask the railway authorities for his jacket, so he chose to sit and shiver in the cold, dark, waiting room. Thinking about what had just happened Gandhi examined how he was mistreated. He was thrown out of the law firm in India because he was Indian, he was thrown out of court in South Africa for wearing his Indian clothes, and now he was thrown out of the train for being in the first class car. He wondered, should he continue on his journey and finish his business in South Africa, or should he just go back home to India? Perplexed, he began to question –what was his dharma? What should he do next? Angered, fearful, and humiliated, Gandhi looked at his feelings as guideposts to reveal what choices he had in front of him. In his autobiography, **An Autobiography: The Story of My Experiments With Truth**, Gandhi expressed his thoughts in that pivotal moment.

"Should I fight for my rights or go back to India," Gandhi wrote. "Or should I go on to Pretoria without minding the insults, and return to India after finishing the case? It would be cowardice to run back to India without fulfilling my obligation. The hardship to which I was subjected was superficial only, a symptom of the deep disease of colour prejudice. I should try, if possible, to root out the disease [of prejudice] and suffer hardships in the process if necessary.... So I decided to take the next available train to Pretoria."

Though contradictory at first, it is in the moment of greatest despair, helplessness, and confusion, that we have the precious opportunity to experience our moment of truth. We have been taught to avoid humiliation and pain. Yet, we have all had these life-changing moments, haven't we? These experiences serve as catalysts that prompt us to make a choice: do we run from the situation, do we accept it and 'just deal with it', do we change the circumstance, or do we change our perspective?

By closely examining our problems with honesty, we are able to see the truth for what it is, and in turn, be true to our Selves.

> **From this place of truth, not only will we see with clarity what action to take, but also, who we truly are in this moment, and what we are made of.**

Every step of the way, we have these choices whenever we are faced with challenges in our lives. In the wee hours of the morning, as the cold South African winds billow in the high altitudes of Maritzberg, Gandhi made a choice that changed the course of history. By introspecting, and discovering that he wanted to change the situation, he knew exactly what to do next. That morning, he decided to take the next train to Pretoria.

Why is it that famous people are always lucky to find their purpose at the opportune moment? They always seem to have that 'Aha!' moment, a moment of clarity, and BOOM! They know what to do! How come that never seems to happen to us? No matter what we do, or who we talk to, we can never get that certainty as to what to do next. Ever had that feeling? So we chug along haphazardly, with our left foot in a boat going one way, and our right foot in another boat going the opposite direction. Pretty soon we jump ship, or fall flat on our faces, wondering what happened!

Before publishing this book, I was happily writing and editing it, when surprisingly, I got admitted into graduate school. I had sent in an application six months prior, mainly because my GRE® (graduate record exam) scores were about to expire. I thought I should at least apply to graduate school so the $200 I had used to pay for the GRE® exams, would not go to waste. Two weeks after receiving my admissions letter, doors were opening up for me without my even asking for it – supportive advisors, paid research, new friends, and on-campus housing. I had graduated from university many years earlier, and for some reason, I had a resistance to pursuing postgraduate education. For me, I thought going to graduate school was giving up my passions – to travel, write, teach, and produce music. Why did I apply to graduate school? What must I do now? After hours of journaling and introspecting, the strangest answer came to me – send in my acceptance letter. A year later, I received my Master's degree in Engineering, and the same question I had before entering graduate school, I came to ask again,

"What's next? Do I stay, do I change my program, do I change my outlook, or do I just leave?"

I felt that I was at the same fork in the road I had happened upon a year earlier! What direction do I want to go? What action do I want to take? What is really the problem – me, or the circumstance? My desire to know what I should do next, consumed me. I talked about it all the time with my friends, my advisors, my mother, my sister, and my brother. I even checked out blogs on the internet, looking for some wisdom to justify an answer inside. But I was afraid of that answer inside. Afraid of the truth. I hid it so well, I forgot what the answer was. Now, there was no recourse, but to dig it up. I'm tired of not knowing where I'm going! My potential is burdening me and weighing me down! I've had enough of hiding from my own truth! No more confusion. No more false sense of feeling overwhelmed and unsure! Time for clarity and wisdom! I'm ready for the Truth to set me FREE!

I hadn't realized that mulling over these questions kept me awake at night. In the moment of realization that I was hiding behind my own excuses of uncertainty, I jumped out of bed. Squinting at my clock, I was shocked that it was 2:38 a.m. I stumbled over to my desk lamp and turned it on. Grabbing my journal, I opened it, and started writing as fast as I possibly could. When the heart is ready, the truth emerges with no disguise. No flowery language. In fact not really many words at all! It was then that I realized the tangible power of looking within your Self for your truth. Confusion, misunderstanding, and the feeling of not knowing where you're going, cannot exist in truth. There is only the present. Only the now. Drop the baggage of the past. Forget the uncertainty of the future. Just be in the stark reality of the moment. And in that moment, is your moment of truth.

I often thought that moments of truth are filled with pomp and glory, trumpets sounding in the skies, letting the whole world know that I *got it!* But, as I look back on those times of assuredness, of inner conviction, of marching to my own drum, they were much like Gandhi's silent decision, in the hallowed sacredness within the depths of his own soul. And that was all there was to it. A sense of contentment, a sense of peace with one's self. A sense of connection to one's truth is renewed, just a little stronger, a little closer, and a little deeper. There is no other secret like this one. No magic spell, no words you can read in books, nor any phenomenon you can discover in the universe, can give you this Truth you seek. For, as the Great Ones say, it can only be found within.

Are you ready for Your Moment of Truth?

It's time for *Secret #2!*

Grab that journal and pen, and let's roll!

Secret #2: Know Your Moment of Truth
Through Introspective Journaling

1. Create your journaling ambience ~ set aside at least **5-7 minutes** for yourself, (no checking email, answering the phone etc.), light candles and incense, and turn on your music player.

2. Play Track 2, *Moment of Truth SoundTrack* from your Discover Your Dharma Soundtrack Album.

3. Turn to a new page in your journal, and write the date, the time, and your location.

4. Practise 1 minute of Stream of Consciousness Journaling. Write super duper fast and don't stop until 1 minute is up. Stay with the excitement of that process.

5. Focus your attention on something that's bothering you right now, or something that you feel is 'missing' in your life at the moment. Whatever it is, write it down.

6. Now, as fast as possible, write down all the things you feel when you think of what is missing in your life, or about anything that happened today that is bothering you.

7. After writing down all your feelings, take a look at what you wrote. Which one jumps out the most? Which ones hurt the most? Which ones scare you the most? Why? Write down why you feel this way.

   Example:
   Why do I feel frustrated and empty? I feel like no matter how hard you try, it's never good enough. That you could do something really well, but it may not make me happy. Or I can do something really well, and I love it, but I don't know how to get paid for it. Things aren't so clear cut for me. I don't just want to go out and get a great job. I want to find something meaningful. But people think I'm a loser if I don't have a 'normal' job. I know I could be creative and work and pursue my passion. But not everything is clicking right away, and the pressure to make money overnight, to be in an amazing relationship, to get moving with what is expected out of life… a lot of pressure for no good reason… and that's what's making me feel like I'm missing something big in my life…

8. Examine what you just wrote. Now, quickly write what statement stands out the most for you? Why?

Example:
The statement that stood out most was the line, " It's something I have no control over." Surrendering and letting go is hard for me to do, that's why this is so scary to me. I don't know how to trust the Universe. I don't know how to enjoy the journey without ending up at the destination I think I should be at. If I don't get the results I'm looking for, I feel like a failure. Wow. This has been a great mirror to see the thoughts I am really thinking! What do I do now?

9. If you are seeking a solution, or an answer to what to do next, ask yourself the following Power Questions™. Notice the first response that comes to mind after each Question. There are no right or wrong answers. They are just guideposts to help you to come to your own Moment of Truth.

   Here is what to do:
   Write the following Power Questions in your journal. As soon as you write the question, quickly write the answer that comes out… *Yes!* Or, *No!*

   Do I want to stay in this situation? ____
   Do I want to leave? ____
   Do I want to change the situation? _____
   Do I want to change myself? _____
   The trick is to answer FAST!
   It works!

10. What do these answers mean to you? What do you think it points you to do now? Write as fast as you can, whatever thoughts come to mind.

11. Look at the answers written clearly on your paper, and see for yourself what you really want to do. *That's Your MOMENT OF TRUTH!*

    Sometimes when we feel we have no choice about a situation we are in, we are in fact choosing to remain stuck. Armed with this new awareness, we now have the choice to do it differently.

    Practice this as often as you can, and notice any patterns, sequences, or habits. Let the answers emerge as you explore deeper.

12. When the music track is over, finish writing your last thought. Put your pen down, and SLAM YOUR JOURNAL SHUT SAYING LOUDLY, "I OWN MY MOMENT OF TRUTH!"

EXAMPLE of Secret #2: Know Your Moment of Truth
Following the above process, Steps 1-8:

March 19, 2009 1:48pm Sitting at my desk.

[Step 4: Stream of Consciousness Journaling for 1 min]
I feel really good, clear, getting things done this week. Gotta keep writing super duper fast until one minute is up... had a great week this week. Just wished I made some time to workout now. I feel I have so much stuff to do....

[Steps 5-6: Focusing on what's bothering me now and how I feel]
What's bothering me now? A lot of things! I am frustrated that I can't find a steady work routine, and finding balance between getting my work done and having fun... too much work, and not enough play! I guess everything is riding on getting a job. I either spend all my time trying to find a job, or wanting to just be my own boss and go for gold with my busi-

ness. I'm stressed out being in limbo, and not making any progress with either...

[Steps 7-10: Power Questions Process]
Do I want to stay in this job vs. self-employed situation? *No!*
Do I want to leave? *Yes!*
Do I want to change the situation? *No!*
Do I want to change myself? *Yes!*

I don't want to stay in this job-no job situation. I want to get out as fast as possible. I don't even care to change it. I know that this is about me... looking for permission from myself to just follow my dharma – it's calling me, to believe, to have faith, to trust, to be willing to hit the grindstone and give my business my all without looking back. And FINALLY! My MOMENT of TRUTH!!! Thank YOU!!!!!

After clarifying what's *really* bothering us, seeing how we feel about it, and then answering the Power Questions, we may have a pretty clear idea what to do next. Whether we have the courage to do it right at this moment or not, that's okay. Just *knowing* what to do next is half the battle! Following through and choosing those consequences is the other half – which will be covered in the upcoming Secrets.

The Power of *Secret #2: Know Your Moment of Truth*

Knowing Your Truth Creates Authenticity

The more you practice this Second Secret, the more of your Authentic Self you will be. When problems arise between yourself and others, you have the opportunity to explore the circumstances, your feelings, and even your inadequacies. Begin to live your life from a place of truth. This can only be done by looking at the truth, and coming from that place of knowing your true Self.

Authenticity is the key to our happiness.

The reason we struggle to know what to do next is that we are not always true to ourselves. In fact, it has been such a long time since we have been honest with ourselves that we have forgotten how to hear our own voice. When we live lives that are incongruent with what our hearts are telling us, we are unhappy. Happiness lies in standing in our own light, with nothing to hide, and nothing to fear. Translucency comes with the willingness to be authentic with our Self, to have congruency with our actions and our values, and to be in alignment with our own wisdom.

Through Introspective Journaling, you will gain the clarity you require to make your own decisions for your life. Not what society wants you to do, or what your family tells you to do, *but what You choose to do.*

We have a tendency to believe that when we do something for others – whether it is a favor, a kind gesture, or an obligation - we do it for them, not for ourselves. What we unwittingly miss is that everything we do, we do for ourselves. If I drop my brother to school, it is not because I have to, but because I choose to - I choose to be a caring big sister, to feel the joy of giving, and to do something that is important to me: to ensure my younger brother gets to school safely and on time. While I did do my brother a favor, I really did it because it is in alignment with my values. As a big sister, I have a perceived role of being this kind of sister to my brother. It has less to do with doing him a favor, and more to do with fulfilling my role as a sister.

How do we extrapolate this idea to bigger 'life' situations? How do we allow our lives to be independent of the choices seemingly imposed on us? For instance, we have to pay the government taxes on April 15, every single year. No matter who you are, you have no choice. But the truth of the matter is you do. You *could* refuse to pay your taxes. You would just have to face the consequences – go to jail, or pay at a later date. You would rather not choose those consequences, so you choose to pay your taxes. See? *We always have a choice.* What if you were in a graduate school in Los Angeles, and your husband gets a job in Hong Kong. You may think, 'I have no choice, I have to quit school and move with him.' But you do have a choice. You could stay in Los Angeles and be apart. However, you may not want the consequence of being apart, so in effect *you chose* to move to Hong Kong with your husband, for you, not just for him.

When we do things for others, it is really for our own selves, for our own reasons.

This means that when you go to school because your parents expected you to, or when you go to work to please your boss or your customers, at the end of the day, *you* chose to do these things… for yourself! We give up the power to make decisions for our own lives by not owning the choices we have made, and the actions we have taken. Why is it so difficult to be rigorous and honest with our Selves? It is because we are expert scheme artists in our own lives. Whatever we want to do, or don't want to do, we make elaborate excuses to justify our actions. 'I really wanted to go to art school, but he said that's not practical. He made me major in computer science instead.' But *we* were the ones who ended up majoring in computer science, not him! So who made that choice? We did! When we blame others for choices we make in our lives, we give up our responsibility for those choices. More importantly, we give our power away.

We no longer feel that we are capable of making choices for our lives, when in fact we have been doing so all along!

Whether it was consciously or unconsciously, we chose the experiences we have had, and the possibilities we have in front of us.

What does this have to do with your dharma? Everything! Imagine if the choices you made were free from the judgment of society, the expectation of your parents, or the fears imposed by your culture? Imagine if you had to answer only to yourself, without limitation or comparison? What if every decision you made were perfect? What would your life look like then? That is the power of authenticity. You are so true to your Self, your highest good, that the constraints of outer expectations and judgments will have no impact whatsoever on what you do, when you do it, or who you choose to be. Be like the swan, gliding gracefully on the lake of inner clarity, unaffected by the squawking and splashing of the ducks around you.

The only way to be truly authentic is to look at our lives squarely in the face, and honestly answer to our Selves.

We may think that by looking at all this dharma stuff, we will have to make big changes in our lives. What we do not realize is that our Moments of Truth are not always about changing what we do, but changing our perspective about it. Remember the story about Gandhi's Moment of Truth? Gandhi had come to South Africa to serve as a lawyer. On his way to the court, he was thrown off the train. That night, he wondered if he should still show up to work the next day, or forget this whole job, and go back to India. In his Moment of Truth, he realized that because of this mistreatment, his perspective shifted. He did not have to give up his job; instead, he still chose to practice law, but now with a new vision. Not too hard to do, right? We think we have to change *everything* to discover our dharma, when, in reality, we might just need to change one little thing.

The Power of Introspective Journaling

Introspective Journaling is a tool to create balance within your self, to see where you are, to create what you want, and to fully realize that everything you seek is already within you.

Introspection is the ability to know yourself so well that your Light cannot be hidden by ugly bad habits or petty behaviors. Just the act of introspection and the conscious effort to cultivate a relationship with yourself, strengthen your soul qualities – truth, peacefulness, radiance, fearlessness, compassion, wisdom, love, and humility. The more your true spiritual qualities are developed, your ego-qualities – victim mentality, blame, pride, jealousy, fearfulness, and ignorance, will wither and fall away. Isn't that cool? So you don't have to work so hard on focusing on your million-and-one bad habits – just practice journaling! The more you journal, the more you are true to your Self!

Ancient psychology is fundamentally based on the study of habits or unwanted behavioral patterns. Lucky for you, through the Power of this Secret, there is no need to work on every single bad habit so that you'll be perfect. *You are already perfect!* Introspection allows you the opportunity to see that all your habits – good and bad – are not really who you are! Just as an angel dressed in rags is still an angel, so you, a divine being, dressed in the rags of your habits and desires, are still untouched by your attire. Introspection into your tendencies or imbalances is an effective way of seeing your habits so clearly, that you will know they are just raggedy clothes, and not you at all! And if you see what you're wearing and you don't like it, take it off and put on something you love! Change your rags of destructive tendencies to the rich robes of your sterling soul qualities. Why pick off every speck of dirt on rags, when you can simply throw it away and step into something enhancing and beautiful?

Introspection calls you to be in integrity with yourself.

Be honest. It's your journal. No one's going to read it. You don't have to create an image. You don't have to be scared someone will judge you. You don't have to impress anyone. You don't have anybody to blame, or anyone to rely on for your breakthroughs. Only you can free yourself. As the saying goes, "The Truth shall set you free." In Introspective Journaling, this is your chance to experience what that truly means.

It is good to talk honestly with yourself in your journal. Sometimes you think you are having successes because you have been busy all day. When you write it all down though, you may see you are just fooling yourself. You were busy doing this and that, and you did not really do anything worthwhile. Other times, you think you are so lazy, you did not do much at all. When you do take a moment to write down all the things you did do, you get to see how much you have accomplished!

If you are still playing hide and seek with your Truth, it is time to stand in your own light! Being a 'scaredy cat' doesn't help you, or anybody else. Pull that pen and journal out, turn to a new page, and go to the first step of *Secret #2* to discover your Moment of Truth!

Your destiny awaits!

Few are those who see with their own eyes and feel with their own hearts.

Albert Einstein, Physicist

SECRET #3

Go Beyond the Line

Spanish painter and sculptor, Pablo Picasso, the co-founder of Cubism, is widely considered the greatest artist of the 20th century. He was unique as an inventor of art forms, as an innovator of styles and techniques, as a master of various media, and as one of the most prolific artists in history. In his lifetime, he produced around 13,500 paintings, 100,000 prints and engravings, 34,000 book illustrations, and 300 sculptures.

Why do we admire Pablo Picasso? If it isn't his staggering number of masterpieces, it would be the fact that he was a revolutionary, an avant-garde, and a non-conformist in everything he did. He was so bold and creative, that despite his reputation, he would go through several years where he painted everything blue, or orange, or red; he would go through inventive phases where all of his art was surrealistic, cubist, or abstract. He was not only radical and rebellious as an artist, but also celebrated, rich, and famous for it too! Even though Picasso was heavily critiqued throughout his entire career, he did not really care. He went on breaking rules in art form and technique, subject matter and style, and anything else he could think of. Everybody knew Picasso was a law unto himself, and he was continuously reinventing himself and his approach to art.

While Picasso is famous for his unconventional art form, you might not have known he was also a surrealistic poet and experimental journaler as well.[2] "I abandon sculpture, engraving, and painting," Picasso wrote in 1936 to friend and poet Jaime Sabartés, "to dedicate myself entirely to song." Over the next four decades, the great artist filled numerous sketchbooks, journals, and even napkins, with surrealistic creations made out of strings of words and characters.

Based on the ideas of André Breton in his *First Surrealist Manifesto,* to "write quickly with no preconceived subject," Picasso wrote in a stream of consciousness manner without any attention to language syntax or semantics. Dating his writings, rather than titling them, Picasso's collection resembled very much what I am about to share in this Third Secret. The aim, for Breton and Picasso, was to bypass literal meaning and allow for one's own self-expression.

Quoted Jaime Sabartés in 1946, Picasso comments on the irregularities of grammar and spelling in his expressive writings: "If I begin correcting the mistakes you speak of according to rules… I will lose my individuality to grammar. I prefer to create myself as I see fit than to bend my words to rules that don't belong to me." Thus were born, the origins of the Wacky Crazy Writing concept.

Picasso was a master of transcending all rules of thought – real and surreal. In the following prose poem, Picasso shares his surrealistic thought flow:

---

[2] Pablo Picasso, *The Burial of the Count of Orgaz & Other Poems*, ed. & tr. Jerome Rothenberg & Pierre Joris (Exact Change)

2 July 38

drop by
drop
hardly
pale blue
dies
between
the claws of
green almond
on the rose
trellis

While writing this Secret #3, I wanted to find a famous personage who could illustrate how journaling out of the box would help you be extraordinary in your own life. As I went through my list of people who had inspired me, I just knew that that person had to be Pablo Picasso. When I Googled "Picasso," all of the websites were about him, or his artwork. In an advanced search on "Picasso writings" what came up in the middle of unrelated links, was an article on a book of collections of Picasso's prose poems translated from Spanish and French, into English. I was both amazed and delighted to see that Wacky Crazy Writing – a technique I made up the night before my first Journaling Funshop™ in 2002, was a reincarnation of an obscure experimental poetry technique Picasso practiced since the late 1930's. Hardly anybone knew about it - least of all me! Consequently, this story brings a sacredness to the Wacky Crazy Secret I am about to share with you!

The night before my first Journaling Funshop, I was on a creative roll. You know how it goes with those 'moments of inspiration' – it was 2 a.m., and I was still printing out the materials to hand out to my first participants the next day. All of the Journaling Secrets were in order in their nice matching binders, and then, I just felt I should do something crazy. I added an exercise with only one rule: THERE ARE NO RULES!!! You just go Crazy! Be wacky! Write wild! Write upside down, inside out, right to up to left to down, in another language that nobody knows, with letters, lines, squiggles, different colors, with your hands, your feet – journal like you never had before! Who cares if there's a point or not – just go nuts! So, I inserted it into the binder with all the other techniques, wondering how it would work out the next day.

I was surprised, no, *shocked* would be a better word, that at my first Funshop, the Wacky Crazy Journaling Technique was a hit! As wacky as it sou nds, it is a whole lot of fun. In every Journaling Intensive Funshop I have had since then, I always plan to have my students do eight minutes of Wacky Crazy Journaling as a break from the intense 'life stuff' throughout the course of the Intensive. When eight minutes are up, nobody wants to stop! After a lot of whining and promises to give up their lunch time, our participants end up doing this for twenty minutes, sometimes half an hour!

There is something liberating and at the same time rebellious, novel, and thrilling about this Wacky Crazy Writing technique. It is definitely a technique that is hard to just read about. It is best to pull out your journal and try it for yourself. I generally don't give any instruction at all. Your imagination is the limit as to how wacky and crazy your pen will be.

The Power of *Secret #3:*
Go Beyond the Line

You might be wondering, "What does this have to do with discovering my dharma? This is a bunch of nonsense!"

And you know what? You're right! It IS a bunch of nonsense – to get you out of the things that you think make 'sense', and into the land of ridiculous unlimited possibilities. The point to remember is this: things will stay the same if you keep doing the same old, same old.

You won't get anywhere until you *go beyond the line.*

Think about it: no matter how exasperated, or ecstatic, or frustrated you feel, you still write left to right, on the line, dotting your 'i's and crossing your 't's'. *You were trained to fit your feelings in between the lines.* I bet in your journal – or any notebook, you don't write over the lines. You don't write across or around the lines. You write *on* the lines, right? Why? Because that's how you were told to write!

So if we were trained to fit our feelings in between the lines, what do you think we'll do when we have ideas, passions, and dreams? We think we have to 'fit' them into the 'lines' too! Not just on paper, but in between the lines created by the structures we live in – our work, family, school, career, business, church, society, country, and whatever other framework we function within. These constraints are no longer parameters for us to dream. Unfortunately, we've allowed these beliefs and judgments of how things 'should' be, become the force that *defines our dreams and how we live our lives. Pretty soon – we begin to think that our lives are the lines themselves!* And then we try to see how best we can 'squeeze in' a little dream, a little hope, a little spark of who we are.

Isn't that the most pathetic thing you've ever heard?

Why live in the narrow constraints of the lines on the paper, the lines of our test scores, the lines of our bank accounts, or the lines in our faces? Why fall prey to those invisible and visible lines that box us in to control how we express ourselves – our feelings, our dreams, and our dharma?

This is your chance to do something wild – go beyond the line! Who wants to be stuck in between the lines? Who wants to be ordinary? Be extraordinary! How do you get out of your oldy moldy ways? How do you bypass your Inner Controller? Just remember Picasso. He was successful because he stayed on purpose with his passion. He didn't bother to think about what was possible or impossible.

Hopefully by now you have a good idea what your Moment of Truth is, right? Now, you have to create new grooves in your brains, and build new neurological pathways in those grooves by doing new things, or the same 'old' things in new ways.[3] Once you start practicing this very powerful technique, you will expand your abilities to reinvent yourself. By practicing this Secret of Wacky Crazy Journaling, you're not only breaking the rules and getting out of your own box, but you get to physically experience what it means to break all the rules in a medium that has been so integrated in the constraints that hold us back. Now, it's time to…

Go Beyond the Line!
Be Wacky! Go Crazy!
Break out of the mold! And Be YOU!

Are you ready to be out of the box, on top of the box, and undeniably EXTRAORDINARY?

Secret # 3: Go Beyond the Line
Through Wacky Crazy Writing

1. Create your journaling ambience ~ set aside at least **8 minutes** for yourself, (no checking email, answering the phone, etc.,), and light your candles and incense.

---

[3] Eriksson PS, Perfilieva E, *et al* (1998) Neurogenesis in the adult human hippocampus. Nature Medicine 4:1313-1317

2. Turn on your music player, and play Track 3, *Go Beyond the Line SoundTrack,* from the Discover Your Dharma Soundtrack Album.

3. Open your journal to a new page. Write the date, the time, and your location.
4. Practice *Secret #1: Wash out the Gunk,* before doing this Wacky Crazy Writing Technique. This will help you to let go of any judgments or apprehension. You want to completely unleash and be able to re-create yourself.

5. Still in the 'writing-super-fast' mode, turn your book 90 degrees so your book is now sideways.

6. Time yourself – give yourself **8 minutes**, or one entire song, to let loose with your pen and journal!
   Don't think, just begin when the music starts. Try to write as crazily as possible – upside down, big, small, in other languages or your own secret language, a bunch of words all in a row, or crazy things that may not make sense in normal syntax. The goal is to make as much nonsense as possible and write out of the norm.

7. All you have to do is put pen to paper and go crazy with words until time is up!

8. Write words next to each other that don't really make sense – e.g. *apple fight with water sitting on a candle singing to my computer hey there crazy words, where you think you fly today? To the moon? To the glue?*
   Write in another language you make up in your head *lae maied fduiogle lie suile quiggle, rufe lia tiggle, giggle fupo lupy.*

Write poems, thoughts, feelings, straight, angular, diagonal, in a circle round and round and then straight, or backwards, or sideways, or with flowers in between – scribble, swirl, twirl, dots, lines, curves, letters, words, whatever you want. The crazier it seems, the better! Use your other hand, your toes, your mouth, anything you feel like.

Try creating rhythms with words, or letters in shapes of what you think matches the sounds. At a Journaling Funshop™, I had a participant who used both hands and his toes - three pens going at once on paper! Sounds crazy? Maybe you could be crazier!

9. The only rule is: NO RULES! Have fun!

10. When the music is over, and you're all done, LOUDLY SLAM YOUR JOURNAL SHUT, AND SAY OUT LOUD "I GO BEYOND THE LINE!"

EXAMPLE of Wacky Crazy Writing done in 8 minutes:

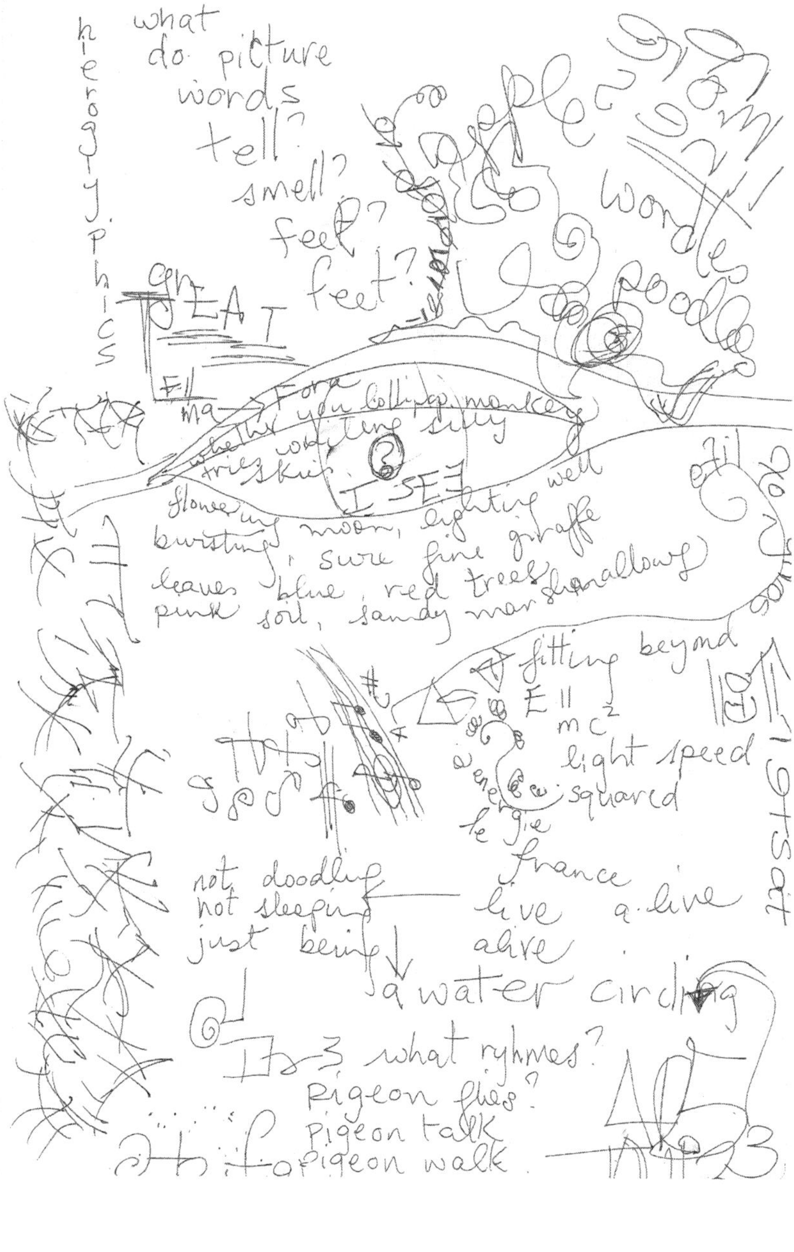

The Power of Wacky Crazy Journaling

The effect you will have is a sense of freedom from the constraints of writing that were imposed on you when you first learned how to write. We were told to write from left to right, and to write in a straight line. Use punctuation. Make sense to the teacher. You'll be graded on what you write. Someone else is judging you. Someone else has to understand what you write. All of these things encroach on you when you come to journal. This technique challenges many of those limitations. With practice, Wacky Crazy Writing gives you the ability to overcome these constraints so that your own voice and self-expression can come out.

When you learned how to write, neural networks related to writing were formed in your brain. Fears, beliefs, and conditioning were also recorded in these networks and even now, they send impulses or reminders when you write. These neural networks were probably never challenged. When you come to write, you bring all of these messages about writing that were created in your brain in 1st Grade. When you journal, you journal in a very rigid, controlled way. Even if you're angry and you just write a string of angry feelings in an irrational way, you still write in a controlled way – from left to right, confined by the space between the lines so you can conserve pages in your journal. Or maybe you have to spell words correctly, or have perfect punctuation, and so on.

Once you start doing this Wacky Crazy Writing technique, you immediately create new neural impulses that will *change those old neural networks forever!* The more you do it, the more it w ill affect not only your journaling, but also your thinking.

Those same old constraining networks not only encroached upon your journaling and writing, they also encroached on your self-expression.

Who says you have to write in a straight line? Who says you have to paint on paper with straight edges, or eat on plates that are round? Couldn't paper be round, or plates be heart shaped, triangular, or irregular?

Wacky Crazy Writing will allow you to tap into your inner creative self, your true voice. These new grooves in your brain are actually new electrical pathways that will affect you on a creative level, and you will begin to approach your life in a new way. You secretly think that by conforming to the norms of society you will be accepted and loved. Maybe there are parts of your self you wished were like everybody else. After Wacky Crazy Writing, think again. You'll start noticing that those same crazy parts of you are what make you, *you*! Not only that, you really begin loving your wild side, and you realize how necessary it is to cultivate this part of yourself. We're all a little bit crazy – we walk crazy, we talk crazy, we dance crazy, we act crazy, so why not journal crazy?

Especially if you feel stuck, this Secret of *Go Beyond the Line* will do wonders. Do this a few times over the weekend and the next week, and you won't have to look hard to see the tremendous power it will have in your life.

Wacky Crazy Writing totally puts the fun in journaling. Have you ever had those days where you think too much about your life? Like, what you should do next, or why things are so complicated right now? Do you ever feel like your mind is going eighteen to the dozen and your head is about to explode? At those times, you may even get to the point where you want to control the results of challenges or decisions in your life. Practice Wacky Crazy Writing to get out of your oldy moldy ways. What a relief - you could bypass your blabbering mind that is ten pages ahead, talking faster than you can write on paper!

Change one tiny part of your life, and you change your energy towards the very part of your life you were stressed out about. As crazy as it sounds, this Wacky Crazy Journaling Technique is really powerful, really simple, easy, fun, and instant. Try it. And enjoy the Crazy You!

This is your moment to give yourself an opportunity to let go. Express your True Self, free from your occasional blithering idiotic mind that controls who you are, wonders what people will think, and tells you that 'this isn't your thing.' If you have an active Inner Critic problem, then please, do yourself a favor, and do this Wacky Crazy Secret. It's time for you to say, "Just Let Me Be!"

Okay, if you are like me and you like to check things out before you do them, I am sure you haven't done this Third Secret yet. So, now is the time to grab your journal, open up to the next clean page, give yourself 8 minutes – put on the music, pick up your pen, and go crazy!

When you are done, turn the page, and let the fun meet your passion for the next Secret in unveiling your Dharma!

Go

beyond

the

line!

STAND OUT!

He who joyfully marches in rank and file has already earned my contempt. He has been given a large brain by mistake, since for him the spinal cord would suffice.

Albert Einstein, Physicist

SECRET #4

Shatter the Myths

World-famous artist and inventor, Leonardo da Vinci, was a legend in his own time, and for centuries to come. With many incredible art pieces in his lifetime, he introduced perspective in art technique, made countless scientific discoveries in anatomy and engineering, and fundamentally impacted art and science forever. He was a visionary, a philosopher, a phenomenal architect, and one of the most innovative engineers of all time. Some say he should have stuck with his art, that it was a pity he did not paint more than he did. But his life purpose was not to paint as much as he could. If it were, he would have. He is an inspiration even to us, centuries later, because he was Leonardo da Vinci, an anomaly to anyone of his time – a genius, and someone who steered his own course, one day at a time.

Da Vinci started out as a great artist who wanted his subjects to look as real as possible. This motivated him to study everything about the human body. And when I say everything,

I mean *everything* – every bodily function, every muscle movement, every body part from the heart to the capillary. In the process he made amazing medical discoveries and developed the scientific method of observation, building the foundation for the study of science as we know it today.

Yet, he did not set out to be one of the world's most renowned scientists. He was just committed to making his art the best it could be, coming up with solutions to improve and redefine the way things were done at the time. The more he exercised that commitment to think 'out-of-the-box,' the more he expanded his consciousness and his ability to apply that approach to anything – from bridge architecture to projectile aerodynamics. He lived his dharma by living each day *on purpose* with the task at hand.

MYTH #1: If I don't stick to what I've been doing for all these years, people will think I'm flaky, a quitter, and unreliable.

TRUTH: Every moment is a new moment. You have the freedom to choose what is right for you now.
Last year you did what was right for you then.
And today you do what needs to be done now.
There is nothing flaky about that.

Da Vinci had this attitude of being on purpose with whatever he was called to do in the moment. As a result, he became a master of whatever path he pursued – his science improved his art, his art improved his study, and his study answered his questions. With his newfound understanding, he created solutions to make the world a better place, striving to make the impossible, possible.

It was *because* da Vinci was an amazing artist, that he was inspired to study cadavers and pursue medical discoveries. Not in spite of his art, but because of it! And that is how it is with everything in our lives. We choose our dharma from moment to moment, taking the right action as opportunities present themselves. The more you journal, the more you will see the connection of events and experiences in your life. Who you are and what you have to offer the world is not in spite of seeming 'confusion' or 'setbacks', but *because* of them.

To be on purpose is to be here in the present moment with yourself and what is in front of you.

We may think that the million-dollar question is, "What do we do now?" But, the real question is, "What keeps us from going forth with confidence and courage? What is it that we are SO afraid of?" The truth is we are afraid of failure and rejection. We are afraid that we are not good enough and that nobody will like us. And we are afraid that if we go after what we want, and fail, we will be a loser for life. Everybody will know it. There is no way of 'deleting' it. We will go down in history as the fool who tried and never made his dreams come true. So what do we end up doing? Nothing. We would rather give up our dreams than be publicly humiliated. We let other people's voices, thoughts, and opinions about our lives, be louder than our own inner voice. Who decides where you should live, what you should do, and who you should marry? Who tells you whether you are successful or not? And, as a matter of fact, who has the right to tell you what kind of life is a 'great life' for you?

We give up the power to make decisions for our lives to our friends, our family, our partners, our teachers, our beliefs, our culture, our society, and our media. Maybe not always directly, but in the constant fear of 'what will people think?' Why are *they* dictating your life? Do *they* know what's best for you? No! You do! How do you know? Because you already have that wisdom inside of you! It's Time for You to live your life – your way! And the only way to do it is by reclaiming your power, and by hearing your own voice.

Why buy other people's beliefs, other people's junk, when you have gold sitting inside... FOR FREE?

We feel we have to 'discover' our dharma because we do not trust that we already know. Secret #4 asks you to *trust that you know.* Trust that you have always known. And trust that you will always know. We hem and haw about going down a certain track, because deep down, we know that we are the ones who keep ourselves back.

When you trust that what you feel is right for you in this moment, then you have won. Because, now you know what to do. When you know what to do, just do it! As long as you do just that, you are on track with your dharma.

The Power of Commitment

The moment you decide to go in a certain direction, commit wholeheartedly to that decision. Fulfill it to the n'th degree in alignment with your personal capacity at this time and space in your life. There is no such thing as waiting to do it later, thinking *"in a couple years things will be different... I'll have more time, I'll have more money..."* – forget it! All you have is *now!*

Commitment is the ingredient that will determine success in the direction you choose.

Even after we have made a decision and have taken action, we want to stay in the 'I'm-checking-this-out-before-I-

REALLY-commit' mode. We are afraid of commitment because we do not want to feel that we *have* to stick with it. But, nothing is wrong with being committed to something at first, and then changing directions later!

MYTH #2: Even though I've made a decision, I don't have to be completely committed to it.

TRUTH: The moment you make a decision, you *are* making a commitment.

If you say yes to something, you are committed to it. It is all in your mind. If you do not believe you have already committed, even after making a decision, then you are being out of integrity with yourself. Once you have made a decision, you have made a commitment. And if you are gung-ho knowing that it is so, you will see a fulfillment of that promise. The more you embrace that, the more you will draw to you opportunities of success! If you do not succeed, make a new decision, and move forward in a new direction!

We have a tendency to think that once we make a decision, we are trapped, and we could never make a different decision after that. Does it really need to be that way? As long as we listen to our intuition and commit to a certain action, the consequences are just what we need – outwardly and inwardly.

Remember, every decision is the right decision. We choose our actions and our reactions. We choose new opportunities to make new choices. Sometimes, life is so hard, we couldn't have possibly chosen this for ourselves. If we always have a choice, why do we make choices that seem to complicate things more than we can handle? It is built into the decisions we make – we choose circumstances that ensure that we grow! If we already passed 1st grade, we would not pick *Dick and Jane* to read every time we have to choose a book. Similarly, as we pass life's tests, our Higher Selves pick more and more challenging circumstances so that we are always progressing. As long as we are growing, blossoming, and flourishing, we are on the right track!

In committing fully to your decision, you attract all manner of things that would not have happened otherwise.

What does it mean to be fully committed? It means to be firm and on purpose in your resolve. It means to do what feels like the right thing for you to do now. Period. Don't wait until you have finished reading this book to start living your grandiose life purpose.

Your dharma is happening in real-time - *now!*
Now! Now! Now!

MYTH #3: I can never be truly happy unless I am living this amazing life that impacts the course of history.

TRUTH: True happiness comes in fulfilling your purpose from moment to moment – your dharma – regardless of outward validation, acceptance, or recognition.

Many of us believe that we are purposeless because we do not fit into the American Dream of the cookie-cutter life – having the right spouse, the successful job, the nice car, and the big house in the suburbs. What is more disturbing is the lackluster of the cookie-cutter life; on the outside, many people have achieved the American Dream, but the reality is: they live 'lives of quiet desperation.' Whether we want the American Dream or not, it is still the standard by which we measure how 'on-purpose' we are with our lives. For some of us, we dream of having that life, and our current lifestyle does not seem to measure up. This is the reason we feel that we are off track, a failure, and can never be enough. For the rest of us, we do not fit the cookie-cutter mold, and do not care for it at all. Yet, by the cookie-cutter metric, we are losers, unsuccessful, and crazy. Whether we follow the metric or not we are still discontented.

The discontent we have with fulfilling our dharma comes from the belief that if we have not done something to impact history, we are nothing. We believe that to discover our life purpose is to discover a secret mission that we were born to do, something that impacts humanity unalterably, and something that is honored and recognized. If we have not achieved that, then we are not on purpose. We have a tendency to feel off-track with our lives, because to be on purpose means to be like the Beatles, Mother Teresa, or Einstein. They are the heroes, and everybody knows them. If we have not gone down in the history books, then we have not lived the extraordinary life we were born to fulfill. But what about the unsung heroes – do we know Mother Teresa's mentor, or Martin Luther King Jr.'s mother? They, like us, are heroes but their names have not made it into the history books, and so we are all 'nothing' – according to our mental definition of 'life purpose.'

We look for outward validation all the time. Look at Rudolph, the Red-Nosed Reindeer. He was perceived as ugly and got beaten up and thrown in a corner by the other reindeer. Then Santa came and said, "Hey Rudolph, that red nose is useful! Won't you guide my sleigh tonight?" Rudolph became Santa's chosen reindeer, and he went down in history! But what if Rudolph did not need Santa to validate him? What if Rudolph knew his light - the gift of his shiny red nose - and felt worthy and useful already?

If we could just accept that we are important to the universe, we would not seek to determine our usefulness and worthiness by the definition of others. It is so easy for us to feel worthless, the scum of the earth, and that our lives are neither here nor there in the grand scheme of things. Shakespeare captured the feeling in his play, *As You Like It,* saying,

> "....Only in the world I fill up a place,
> which may be better supplied when I have
> made it empty."

Isn't that how we feel about ourselves, sometimes? We walk around like human robots – wake up, eat, listen to the news, hop in the car, zoom off to work, run around all day, come home, microwave some food, check our email, watch some TV, and roll into bed. Only to do it all again tomorrow! Is that why we are here? Couldn't someone else do the same thing we do? What is so special about us?

> **It is not about what you do, it is about who you are! You have a role in the universe, or else you would not be here.**

What is that role? To be the best you can be in this moment! How do you know that in the next moment, you will still be here? Look at the sudden life-changing disasters that plague the human existence, from the tsunami in Thailand to 9/11 in New York City. We do not know what the future holds for us. If you are the best you can be in this moment then you have discovered your dharma. Take action on what is presented to you from moment to moment. Why do we think we have to be a certain 'age' before we are on purpose with our lives? Why can't it be *now?* The fact that we are here means that we are contributing to the universe.

We are part of the universe, and whatever we contribute is a critical part of sustaining this creation – we must never feel that we are not on purpose!

As Max Ehrman captured in his poem, *Desiderata,*

You are a child of the universe. No less than the trees and the stars. You have a right to be here. And whether or not it is clear to you, the universe is unfolding as it should.

How *do* we figure out our dharma? If this whole cookie-cutter thing is a sham, what is the real deal? Most of us want to know the end result before we start the journey. We miss the traveling because we are so focused on the end.

The point of the journey is not the destination.
It is to experience the journey itself.

What does that mean? It means that the time we spend doing, thinking, feeling, and being – is the point of our life! That's our journey. *That is our dharma.*

Our dharma unfolds every day that we live, a conglomeration of our perspectives, our beliefs, our choices, and our actions, which all add up to… us! Do we do things just to get things done in the world, or do we do things so that we can grow, give, beckon, and receive? Are we on the planet just to 'get through life,' or are we here to *experience* life? We are here to receive the gifts life has to offer us and to ensure that *we* learn, *we* grow, and *we* transform.

The Socratic Approach

Asking questions help you to be on purpose. Discovering your dharma starts with wanting to know the answers to these questions. The amazing effect of the Socratic Approach is to get an answer by the process of questioning, and to experience a realization that you knew the answer all along; that you have all the answers within.

When I started out on this quest to figure out what I want to do with my life, I was really frustrated, miserable, and clueless. In a sense, it was good for me because I became so fed-up with this irksome sense of discomfort I knew it was getting in my way. Feeling discontented in the middle of a long day in the lab, I turned to the back of my lab notebook and began to write: *"I really am tired of being frustrated and miserable. Why don't I know what to do with my life?"* And the next sentence just came right out – *"I know what I want to do with my life. I want to write books. I want to play music. I want to travel, and I want to get paid doing these things!"* Without skipping a beat, another question popped out – *"Yeah, so how WILL you do that?"* And that is how it all got started. Socratic dialoging – with myself, my pen, and a piece of paper.

Has anyone ever asked you an insightful question which made all the difference? Maybe it was your teacher, your mom, your partner, or even a stranger. Maybe it was a seemingly innocuous question – "What's up?" Or, maybe you were the person to ask them a question, and all of a sudden, they got it! They knew the answer! We have all experienced one of those light bulb moments.

What do you do when you have too many things on your plate, and you are not sure which one is the right thing to pursue now? Whenever you have a major problem figuring out: what to do, in what order, to what capacity, and where to begin, you can use the Socratic Approach. The process of Secret #4, takes all the options you want to pursue, from the broad to the specific, and helps you see with more clarity what you want to do first.

Mindblowing, isn't it? *It's only Secret #4, and this is the moment you've been waiting for, right?*

> **Socratic Journaling is the process of question-and-answer, or self dialogue, through the magic of your pen.**

Are you ready? Great! As we discover how to shatter the myths that hold us back, we get to ask ourselves the 'big' questions and tap into that nagging sense of discontentment that seems to haunt our souls. Remember how frustrated I got sitting in my lab, that I just started writing out questions? Remember the part where the answers seemed to pop up through my pen? That is exactly what we are going to do! You don't have to worry if you are asking the right question or not. Any relative question to the issue will lead you to the answer you need.

IT'S TIME TO SHATTER THE MYTH!

Secret #4: Shatter the Myth
Through Socratic Journaling

1. Create your Journaling Ambience – set aside **10-15 minutes**, for this experience. Turn on your music player, and grab your journal and pen. Play Track 4, the *Shatter The Myths SoundTrack,* from your Discover Your Dharma Soundtrack Album.

2. Take a deep breath, and release all the tension from your body as you let your breath go. Feel a tingling peace as you breathe deeply again. Now breathe out, this time deeper than before. Just relax and breathe deeply once more, and let it go.

3. Feel the magic of the moment. Set the intention that what is meant for you to experience now, will be revealed to you.

4. Open your journal to a new page, and write the time, the date, and your location.

5. Writing super fast for 1 minute, get the pen flowing with a quick sprint of Stream of Consciousness Journaling. Just write, don't stop. The purpose is to do a quick clearing out of any gunk on your mind.

6. Still in super-duper-fast mode, take 1 minute to write down all the things you want to pursue at this moment. That's right - anything that comes to your mind, write it down – FAST!

   Example:
   Live shows with my band, script-writing, freelance web-consulting, travel the world, photography, live in Europe….

7. Now, using the first one you wrote down, ask yourself, *"Why am I choosing to pursue this?"*
   See what answers come up for you. Write them down.

   Example:
   Why did I pick 'Doing live shows with my band'?
   I love playing music, writing music, and having fun with my band. I feel high on life, pumped up, and in the moment. I love

everything about it – being creative, jamming with my band-mates, getting gigs, and making money having a blast! I could play music forever – it is so much fun and fulfilling!

8. Ask another question based on your answer, so you can go deeper into this thread. Or, you can ask another question you always wanted to ask, like:

- ***Is this in alignment with what I'm passionate about? Should I ditch my band and go to the East Coast for this program or not?***
  I really love my band, earning money, and having new opportunities to expand. But somehow, it feels right to go to the East Coast for this program – I don't know why! Who knows? I'll meet cool people in the program, and something amazing will emerge. If anything, I will learn a lot, and be able to have a lot more opportunities because of it!

- ***What if school is just an excuse to put off getting around to going big with my band?***
  Yeah. The problem is I tend to plan so much, I'm afraid I'll get nothing done at this rate. I think I have to be more and more qualified to play on bigger stages. The truth is there is no way to know what you're doing until you go out there and just do it. You determine your own worth!

- ***What does your heart tell you?***
  Go for it. It's all your life. You don't have to figure out how it all plays out. This is what you want to do now. So why not? Go be yourself and make the most of it. It's not about school. It's about making what you need, to be available to you. Learn. Have fun. Be creative...

9. When you're done asking questions on the first thing, (in this example, *Live shows with my band),* pick the next

thing you can pursue, and repeat Step 7. (NOTE: The process in Step 7 is called **Funneling.)**

10. After you've funneled ALL of the things you want to pursue through this process, rank them in priority starting with which one you want to pursue first, second, third, etc. What do you want to do now? Which ones can you pursue at the same time? List your Top 4.

    Example:
    We started out with:
    Live shows with my band, script-writing, freelance web-consulting, travel the world, photography, live in Europe....

    And ended up with:
    Funnel Rankings outcome -
    1. *Record music*
    2. *Attend Script-Writing Program / Web-consulting*
    3. *Live in Europe and travel/ photography when I travel*
    4. *Live Shows with Band/ Make mini-music videos*

    Pretty clear, right? Sometimes you may know exactly what feels right in this moment. You can explore it a bit, and if it still feels right, pursue it. With the new funnel rankings Top 4, you have a working outline of a clear plan to follow. Isn't that cool?

11. When you are done exploring your funnel rankings, SLAM YOUR JOURNAL SHUT, AND DECLARE LOUDLY, "I KNOW WHAT TO DO NEXT!"

If you are one of those people who are so excited about a lot of things, and could see yourself going in many directions, this funneling thing may seem a bit overwhelming. Relax. It is okay if you are having a hard time with this exercise. It could take a little while to get the hang of it, but after 2 or 3 funneling rounds, you will be a pro for sure. It was a little tricky for me too at first, which is why I am mentioning it here. It is not the journaling; it's our own fears - our fears of commitment to who we are, and the fear that we don't have any excuses anymore. Why? Because once we know what makes our hearts sing, we can't go back to mozying around being miserable and hiding from our Light.

It's strange how we can actually do that to ourselves – hold on to our excuses at the cost of our own happiness. These excuses are the Real Myths we want to SHATTER! Luckily, there is a little easier twist with Socratic Journaling that can help you get around this unhelpful tendency. I have to say, you have no excuse but to keep at it! Don't give up! I believe in you - you can do this! And YOU DESERVE IT! YOU DESERVE THE AMAZING DESTINY THAT AWAITS YOU!

Maybe the following example can help you get started. Once you get into the swing of things, you can go back and follow the Funneling Socratic Process. Breathe and let go... Be open to all the exciting possibilities that are about to be revealed to you. Sounds good?

You can copy the questions, and see what answers come up for you. Or, you can write your own questions as they emerge. Write by hand... the questions *will* emerge. And so will the answers!

EXAMPLE:

"I don't know what question to ask. Why?"

(Take 3 deep breaths.) I hate these questions! This is lame! I have no life. I have no friends. I'm totally broke. I feel like a loser. I don't like where my life is going, and I don't want to think about it right now.

"Why don't I want to think about it right now?

(Take 3 deep breaths.) I don't want to think about it right now, because I'm scared. I'm scared that if I do what I really want, I won't

make any money to be able to live. I'm scared people won't talk to me. I'm scared of even getting my hopes up because I'm scared I will lose the little money I have in the bank. And I will be even more of a loser. I'll remember how things aren't that great and then I'll be sad.

"Why would I be sad?"
(Take 3 deep breaths.) I feel like life is passing me by. I feel like I'm not getting anywhere. I'm sad because I'm not motivated to do anything different about my life. I don't know anybody cooler to be friends with. I can't find a better job. I don't have the time to do the things that make me happier. I just get bummed out on it all. Nobody cares.

"Why do you think that nobody cares?"
(Take 3 deep breaths.) I feel nobody knows what I'm going through, or support me in being better. I don't know - I'm just so frustrated at myself. I'm smart, I have the ability, I know what to do, I just forget what the point is, and then I don't do anything. I guess I wait till the pain factor is so great, it'll motivate me to get up and do something because I can't take it anymore. And if I don't care, why should anybody else care? But I don't want to do that. I want to be happy now. I want to have joy and peace. I want to do the things that make me happy. I want to be motivated by touching people's lives. I want to be somebody. I want to be known as a great musician, a great thinker, a great inspiration to others.

See how it goes? There's nothing to it. Once you start writing, the next question will emerge. The little secret to it too, (I'm not sure if Socrates would approve) is the 3 deep breaths after asking each question. Breathing helps oxygenate your heart and mind, and deep exhalations help release tension, anxiety, and self-criticism. Also, go with the flow. When you open your eyes and you feel an answer emerging, keep writing. Go beyond the sentence; tap into the feeling and the feeling behind that feeling. And BREATHE! Breath will lead you through your feelings and thoughts to a place of deeper clarity and underderstanding. Your pen will guide you as you journey through the land of your fears and feelings.

The Power of Socratic Journaling

With Socratic Journaling, you have the opportunity to ask your Self any question, and get the answers you need. You have just learned the powerful steps to effective Socratic Journaling so you can find out how to know what you really want to do next in your life.

Why does Socratic Journaling work? We seek enlightenment to get out of our darkness. Answers enlighten us. Answers expand our consciousness to embrace our wisdom and our truth. By asking questions and allowing our pens to write, we are giving our hearts the chance to talk. The more we practice Socratic Journaling, the louder that voice becomes. Throughout the day, we do hear our hearts. It is just that our heart's voice is very faint – so faint that we do not believe it is our heart. We doubt, and we search for answers on the outside. When we get the answer, we often forget that it was the same answer we had all along. Imagine if we knew a person who claimed to be a psychic. She prophesies, but we do not believe her at first. As her prophesies come to pass, we are able to verify she was telling the truth, and the more instances we verify, the more we believe her. Soon, whatever she says will happen, we believe. That is the power of Socratic Journaling – the power of believing in your own intuition.

Through the process of Socratic Journaling, you are strengthening your complete trust in your heart's wisdom. In looking back at your journal entries, you can begin to observe your intuitive hunches, and verify their validity. The process of journaling is a way of consciously drawing on your heart's wisdom. Your journal will soon show you how often your intuition has guided you in your life.

The power of Socratic Journaling is the gift of a question In our experiences - schooling, interviews, dates, relationships, and business, questions have a judgmental undertone. We have lost the true meaning of asking a question. Instead of using questions as a means of getting information to enlighten us, we use questions as a means of judging others. Socratic Journaling is very simple and instantly effective. Yet, it is sometimes the hardest process for my Dharma Express® participants, and it requires the most time and effort to practice. Why? The reason is we are afraid of questions. We see questions as accusations we have to disprove. When our teacher asked us a question in school, we felt that we had to prove how smart we were or that we had to know the answers. If we did not know the answer, we would feel ashamed, and beat ourselves up over it. We also believed other students would think we were stupid and incompetent. As grown-ups, if we ask someone a question about who they are or how they feel, they get defensive as a result of their past experiences. They never give you a straight answer. Do you ever notice that about yourself?

What if, for a moment, you suspend the belief that questions cause pain? What if a question were asked out of the desire to simply know the answer? Notice after this session, how your method of inquiry shifts. You might start asking with the expectation of getting an answer, to be enlightened. At first you might not get there. That's okay. We all experience this when we first start the process. Keep practicing it whenever you get a chance. Soon you will begin to see a question as an expression of sincere curiosity.

This process of asking questions out of curiosity will continue beyond the few minutes you spend with your journal. As you begin living with a new sense of wonder and intrigue with the world around you, something very magical happens: you begin living in the moment.

> **Inner delight for discovery cannot be bound by the pages of your journal.**

Take the discoveries from your journal, and practice them in your daily life. You will feel this curiosity as you eat your breakfast, as you look out the window to see the clouds, or as you notice that you hum the same tune when you open the refrigerator. Every moment is a brand new moment.

Remember Leonardo Da Vinci? You don't have to figure out everything in one funneling session. You don't have to know how it will all play out. *Follow your passion, and trust the discovery process.* Life is ever changing and surprising. Why do you want to be an Excellent Funneler? Because you're going to be doing it for the rest of your life! There are always things to funnel – new visions, new directions, new things to pursue, and many new passions.

> **The funnel helps you to have clarity when you are overwhelmed or confused; it helps you to prioritize and know where to direct your energy.**

Funneling, or the Socratic self-dialoging process, is one of the greatest tools of journaling you could master. At the Discover Your Dharma Intensive, we make sure you really get this. I know for me, it is really important to be able to go from "Ok, I sorta know what I'm passionate about, and I have about 10 things I could pursue..." to " I know I have a lot of things I want to do, but all I have to do is _____ right now." Once you narrow things down a bit, you will clear out a lot of confusion concerning what path to pursue next in your life.

After Socratic Journaling you will begin to have a new perspective as to how things are shaping up. If you're feeling a little shaky about how you're going to take this next step, fear not! Secret #5 shows you how to follow your heart *no matter what!* You will want to make sure you're doing the right thing for the right reason. It's time you feel that knowing deep down in your heart. After the short break, we'll come back to dive into an exciting experience of "how you really know for sure" what the next step is for you.

Right now, let's change the energy. Stand up. Streeetch your arms way into the sky. Stand on your tipee-toes and reach...reach for the stars. Wiggle your fingers and shake your arms and feet. Roll your head from left to right to relax your neck. This Secret had a lot, I know. Great job for rolling with it! You're awesome! It's hard to read a book that tells you that it doesn't have the answers to your life - only you do! I'm here to share with you how you can find your own answers. That's what these next Secrets will reveal to you. Feel the power of your own truth, and hold on to it!

You are your own best expert!
Be the Master of Your Life!

We'll see you after the break for the most exciting transformation you will experience. The hardest part is over! Now, the *real* fun begins! Are you ready for the Advanced Secrets #5 through #10? In this next phase of discovery you will learn how to follow YOUR Dharma in real-time!

How will you choose to fulfill your Destiny?

A Special Quote on Commitment...

W. H. Murray writes in **The Scottish Himalaya Expedition, 1951**:

'But when I said that nothing had been done I erred in one important matter. We had definitely committed ourselves and were halfway out of our ruts. We had put down our passage money and booked a sailing to Bombay. This may sound too simple, but is great in consequence.

Until one is committed, there is hesitancy, the chance to draw back, always ineffectiveness. Concerning all acts of initiative (and creation), there is one elementary truth the ignorance of which kills countless ideas and splendid plans: that the moment one definitely commits oneself, the providence moves too. A whole stream of events issues from the decision, raising in one's favor all manner of unforeseen incidents, meetings and material assistance, which no man could have dreamt would have come his way. I learned a deep respect for one of Goethe's couplets:

Whatever you can do or dream, you can begin. Boldness has genius, power and magic in it!'

Begin Your Expedition!

Sometimes the questions are complicated and the answers are simple.

Dr. Seuss, Author

SECRET #5

Follow Your Heart No Matter What

To many, Mother Teresa is an icon of peace and compassion, feeding the poor, taking care of the unwanted, the dying, and the downtrodden. But to me, her greatness lies in her unwavering courage to follow her intuition no matter what. The life she led was definitely not an easy one; every step of the way, she listened to her intuition, and took action despite all odds.

What was her secret? How could she listen to her inner voice, and have the guts to follow through, even when people forbade her, scoffed at her, and didn't believe that she could?

Sometimes we think that to live our grandiose dharma, we have to have some exotic extraordinary vision and some secret plan to get there. And if we don't know what the plan is, we can't take action, because we feel we don't know where we're going. That's why we're doing this Discover Your Dharma Intensive, right? We want to figure out our Master Plan! But do you think Mother Teresa of Calcutta at the age of seventeen, said, "You know what? I'm going to chart out my life's path. I'm going to defy the rules of the Convent, be a rebel nun, start my own order, open my own orphanage, win the Nobel Prize for Peace, and become a revered saint?"

Nope. She just did what felt like the right action to take in the moment. From moment to moment, she strived to live consciously, helping the unwanted, the forsaken, the sick, the poor, and the dying – no matter what.

Similarly for us, we have the ability to *follow our hearts no matter what*. For each of us, our lives are made up of all the moments we have lived, the choices we have made, and the experiences we have drawn to ourselves. For Mother Teresa, her life was one that touched millions through 70 years of love and service to humanity – just by living her dharma. In being present with her inner voice, and in doing whatever she was called to do one day at a time, Mother Teresa was fulfilling her destiny. She didn't know what the future would look like, who she would become, or how her work would expand; but she *did* know that what she was doing in the moment was the right thing, and that's all there was to it.

People told her on countless occasions, "You can't do this, you can't go in the gutter and save the world, and *still* be a nun. That's crazy!"

So deep was her trust in her intuition and her convictions, Mother Teresa was undaunted.

How many times have you heard successful people say, "The reason I'm successful today is that I was in the right place at the right time. I just felt the impulse to talk to that person, and it turned out to be the best move I ever made." Have you ever wondered why it happened like that? Most times we think, "Gosh, they were so lucky!" We rarely stop to wonder about the happenstance of it all. What is it that guided them to just follow that hunch to make that 'lucky' call, or talk to the 'right' person? More importantly, do we, the 'unlucky' ones, wait for that moment of inspiration, or do we create it at will for ourselves? Why should the 'lucky' ones get to live their dharma, while we unfortunate souls live in tortured limbo?

Are you ready for the answer? Yes?

GREAT! Today is your lucky day!

The Secret to Following Your Heart

I know from my own life, it is tricky to follow the heart. Why is it so hard? The reasons are:

1. You have to be able to *hear* your heart,
2. You have to trust that it *is* your heart (and not your super-ego or your fears), and
3. You've got to have the courage to follow your heart's wisdom, knowing it is the right thing, no matter what.

Each of these steps is a bit fuzzy on their own, much more to put them all together into one action: follow your heart.

Some people can hear their heart, and the more they practice following their heart, the easier it is for them to listen to it. As a result, they are stronger in following their heart's wisdom, even if it is hard, or crazy, or simply straightforward. However, for those of us who have trouble hearing our inner voice, or second-guess it a lot, where do we start? Wouldn't it be helpful if we could eliminate our fears that come up just when we were about to listen to that inner voice? What if there were some special secrets to bypass our programmed inner critic and allow our heart's voice to come through?

If you think going straight to the heart would be a good idea instead of all of those highfalutin intellectual labyrinths, then you are ready for **Secret #5!**

Secret # 5: Follow Your Heart No Matter What
Through Non-Dominant Hand Journaling

1. Create your journaling ambience ~ set aside at least **15 minutes** for yourself, (no checking email, answering the phone etc.,) and light a few candles and incense.

2. Turn on your music player, and play Track 5, *Follow Your Heart SoundTrack* from the Discover Your Dharma Soundtrack Album.

3. Turn to a new page in your journal, and write the time, date, and your location.

4. Think of a difficult decision or a challenging situation you're going through in your life right now.

5. Write it down, and write any questions you want to ask about what you're experiencing right now. If a question or a situation doesn't come to mind, here are some you can start with (just write down one question in your journal for now):
   What should I do about this?
   Why is this so difficult?
   What do I really want to do?
   Why do I want to do this?
   Why do I feel unsure?
   What shall I do with my life?
   What makes me happy?
   What am I passionate about?
   What are my gifts to share with the world?
   What was I born to do/give?
   What should I do now?
6. After you write the question, quickly put your pen in your *non-dominant writing hand,* (the hand you *don't* usu-

ally write with) and write whatever answer comes up. If you're not ambidextrous, it will be a little hard to write with your other hand. Don't worry if you can't write fast, or if it's scratchy and big. It's ok. Watch your journal become your crystal ball. Fully trust in this experience.

7. Now, in your regular writing hand, write another question, either from your heart, or from the list above. Switching the pen back to your non-dominant hand, write as fast as possible, what you want to say in response to that question.

8. Continue back and forth with new questions, and observe yourself experiencing the process.

9. When the music is up and you're all done, put your pen down. Slam your journal shut and say loudly "I FOLLOW MY HEART NO MATTER WHAT!"
   Feel the tingling sensation throughout your body. Close your eyes and breathe deeply.

Journaling Tip:
As soon as you write the question, put the pen in your non-dominant hand, and immediately start moving the pen on paper, allowing the answer to flow through. The speed will circumvent your mind wanting to tell you what the answer should be.

EXAMPLE of Non-Dominant Hand Journaling:

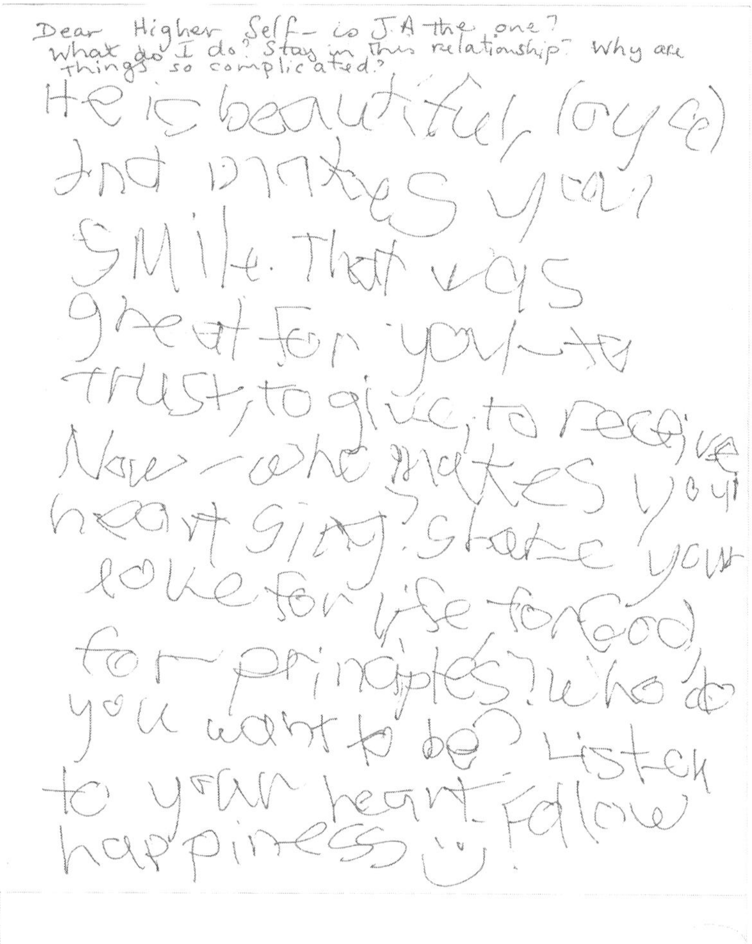
Dear Higher Self - is J.A the one? What do I do? Stay in this relationship? Why are things so complicated?

He is beautiful, loving and makes you smile. That was great for you to trust, to give, to receive. Now - who makes your heart sing? Share your love for life, for God, for principles? Who do you want to be? Listen to your heart. Follow happiness

No need to tell your hand what to write. Your Higher Self already has the answer. As you write, you will see that your handwriting is jagged, big, and scraggly. You may need to turn the journal sideways so your hand can have enough space to write your words. At first, the words are big and hard to read - much like a 1st grader struggling to write. Be patient. Keep breathing, and lovingly allow your Higher Self to feel safe in taking its time to talk with you. Part of this process is to surrender and have no judgments. Just as you would excitedly let a 4-year-old take his time to write, allow your Inner Self to write however long it takes for it to form the letters and to finish a word. Your hand might hurt a little or get tired quickly because it is not used to writing. Give yourself a rest in between questions. *The power is in the non-dominant hand.*

The Power of *Secret #5: Follow Your Heart No Matter What*

You will find that your Inner Self knows exactly what is going on, what you are afraid of, and what you need to do. I am always amazed at how direct my Higher Self is with me. Sometimes I mull over situations to death and cannot seem to hear my inner guidance. Even worse, I drive everybody else crazy in the process.

A perfect example is an experience I had when I had just graduated from graduate school. I chose not to pursue a PhD because I realized that I wanted to pursue other things that I felt I had to do *now*. Like publishing this book, giving seminars, and helping people find their dharma. While I had my moment of truth, and *knew* what to do next, I wasn't sure if I had the courage to just walk away from the PhD program. I started to think – I had already made it this far, what's a few more years to go? Instead of completely leaving the program, I decided to apply for a leave of absence. This way, I wasn't enrolled, but I wasn't totally gone from the program either. As one semester rolled into the other, I kept on renewing my leave until there were only a few weeks left before I finally ran out of leave. I had to make a decision – do I leave the program, start my business, and publish my book? Or do I play it safe and just enroll in the program anyway? I tried not to think about it. Even though I was focused with my work, I was extremely sensitive and irritable. I *knew* I was not listening to my heart. I kept telling myself, *"I don't have TIME to journal. I don't have time to meditate. I have so much stuff to do – I don't have time to breathe! I really don't have time to sit for a moment... I just don't feel like dealing with this right now. I'll figure it out later."*

Yeah right. Every time a friend stopped by, I unloaded all my troubles, dilemmas, and self-dialogue. Pretty soon, all of my friends had heard the same story, and after a month, they were beginning to get tired of it. Eventually, they started telling me they don't want to hear it anymore, just do whatever I want. And you know how it is, when you are asking others' advice, the *last* thing you want is somebody telling you, "Do whatever you want." That was when I knew I kept looking 'out there' for a sign, and I was scared to look inside. Why was I so scared to follow through on my Moment of Truth? I am the Dharma Journaling Expert, and I know the tools, the psyche, and the excuses. So why don't I just sit for a moment and do Secret #5?

In that moment I realized the second part to Secret #5. It is not so scary to 'follow your heart.' The scary part is to 'follow your heart *no matter what!'*

We have gotten used to ignoring our inner voice for our entire lives. As a result, we have developed the habit of ignoring the familiar nagging sense of discontentment or intuition. Now when we *want* to hear our inner voice, and we *want* to follow through on it, for some reason, we don't. That is because we have these neurological grooves in our brains that trigger the 'ignore response.' How do we undo these grooves, and break the habit of ignoring our inner voice? How do we stop coming up with excuses that keep us from following through no matter what?

To help unravel your wisdom through the chaos of your mind, practice this Non-Dominant Hand Journaling Technique for 5 minutes, as often as possible. It will bypass your mind's inner critic that is always full of brilliant excuses. Practicing this Secret will make your inner voice so loud and clear, it will be impossible to ignore.

I was scared to acknowledge what my heart was saying, because I didn't think I had the courage to do what it said. In a moment, I had fallen prey to my 'old ways' of going with the flow and not really taking charge of my life. But my inner voice was too loud to ignore. I knew the only answer was to be committed to that truth. I'm in charge of becoming who I want to be, and how I choose to express myself in the world.

Here is the Secret to live your life on purpose: follow your heart no matter what.

Why wait for something dramatic like an accident, an illness, or a mid-life crisis to give you a painful wake-up call? Why not wake-up *now?* Practice these 10 Secrets! If you are the logical and analytical type, go all out for five minutes with this Non-Dominant Hand Journaling Technique. Just listen for a moment and you will know that your Wisest Self has all the answers.

Culturally, we have been trained to turn to other people for answers when we are unsure of ourselves. I have an elderly friend who has it all figured out – whenever she is overwhelmed, or feels unsure about what to do about 'big' decisions, she would call up the minister.

"Brother, what should I do next?" She would ask. "Should I do this or that?"

While it is enlightening to talk to your minister, your mom, or your best friend about what to do next, you end up strengthening your trust in *their* wisdom, instead of your own! The 'complicated' choices we have to make – whether it is to stay in a relationship or to find a new job - is not really about making the best decision. It is about getting a chance to follow our hearts! We get caught up in thinking about all the possible consequences, and we forget that it is not about those things at all! It's about us! *Here is our chance to grow! Here is a chance to listen to our hearts! Here is a chance to realize who we truly are, and what we were meant to become!* How will we grow if we keep shrinking when these difficulties come our way, passing it off to someone else? Every time we avoid the hot and sticky situations, every time we have the chance to follow our hearts, and don't... we are missing our chance to grow stronger, wiser, and happier. Why is that? The truth is: our transformation occurs by standing in the heat under immense pressure.

The diamond – famous for its exquisite beauty and unparalleled strength – is actually highly organized carbon formed under tremendous pressure and heat. The *pressure* and the *heat* are the key factors that turn carbon dioxide into diamonds. And it is not just a little pressure and a little heat, but 725,000 pounds of pressure per square inch, and a smoldering 2200 degrees Fahrenheit that are continuously sustained by a trapdoor made out of 100 miles of the Earth's crust! Over billions of years, the carbon then rushes to the Earth's surface to cool, forming the extraordinary diamond – a unique crystal structure that is the strongest material in the world.

Transformation comes from standing in the heat and becoming finer, stronger, and better as a result.

The more we build the muscles of following our intuition, the more we are fulfilling our dharma. If you have a pressing issue in your life where you need some insight and direction, pick up your pen in your non-dominant hand, and start writing. Ask any question. Your Higher Self knows you better than you do. It knows what the real questions are. And it knows the answers.

In every situation, who you are is more important than what you do. My friend, Michelle, is a high school teacher.

Within her first month of teaching, she had a challenging situation where one of her students, Alex, made a racist remark to one of the other students. Things soon got out of hand, and Alex was suspended from school for a week. When Alex returned, the class ostracized him, which only made matters worse. Soon, Alex was Michelle's nightmare – he seemed to cause trouble no matter what. With a volatile classroom, Michelle was at a loss as to how to regain control of her class, and she felt that she was always fighting an uphill battle. Michelle was constantly preoccupied with Alex, and the belief that Alex was ruining her class. It was not long until Michelle was a basket case, barely holding herself together. Finally, after a million and one tactics, she asked me, "How do you handle challenging situations in your classroom? What do you do that I can do too?"

The crux of the matter: it is not about what you do; it is about *who you are*. We have all heard that line a thousand times, but in a society driven by results, there is only time for doing, not being. And that is exactly my point: *being and doing are not the same thing!* Alex 'happened' to Michelle, in a sense. Not for Michelle to see what more she can do on the outside, but for her to awaken, and to realize who she has to *become* in order to rise to the challenge. When Michelle realized that, she saw that she needed to stand up for herself, to claim her own power as a teacher, and to forgive Alex and herself. Many times, we don't need an answer that tells us what to say, or what to do next, but a true awakening, a clarity that will open our eyes to the jewel behind the lesson: what we are being called on to become.

Challenges happen to us on the outside *so that we can transform on the inside.*

If only we allow that transformation to happen! If not, those same old challenges will follow us around, until we do transform! How wonderful! So if we get scared, make a mistake, or miss the point, we need not worry. That challenge will come to us until we take heed, get the point, and move on! So, what keeps us from 'getting the point'? What makes us afraid of staying in the heat, standing under the pressure, and following our hearts no matter what?

From epic legends to fairy tales, we have been inundated with the idea that there is a formula to follow our heart. If we are stubborn and resistant, we think the formula is to do things the hard way despite what anyone says. We must face trials and tribulations – they are a sign that we are listening to our inner voice. We make things intricately complex for ourselves, and have so many repercussions to deal with, that we hardly have time to be clear-cut and follow our intuition. According to many epic legends – from Hercules to Frodo and the Fellowship of the Rings, our formula fits: things must be difficult in order for us to follow our heart. When things are flowing, and miracles are happening, we say to ourselves, "Nahhh. This can't be! It's coming too easy! This can't be it!" Have you ever sabotaged a good thing going for you? Have you ever had doors open right in front of you, and you run the other way? Practice Secret #4 and Secret #8. These techniques will reveal how often you complicate things on a daily basis, and how to get rid of this self-sabotaging tendency once and for all!

Then there are other times where we are afraid of failure and we lack the zest to persevere. At these times, it is convenient to apply the fairy tale formula where everything has to be perfect in order for us to follow our heart. If we face challenges, obstacles, or troubles, we think they are life's way of telling us that we are going in the wrong direction, and that we are not listening to our intuition. Only when everything is falling into place and things are all rosy, we feel, "Aha! See? Now everything is working out. I am ready to listen to my heart!"

To follow your heart, there are no black-and-white rules; it does not have to be the easiest way, or the hardest thing.

Life does not have to be 'perfect' to confirm that we are following our intuition. If in this moment, your intuition is guiding you to do something fun and easy, go for it it! If at this moment, your heart is guiding you to do something difficult and challenging, do it! If your intuition is guiding you to take action now, even though all the circumstances aren't perfect, do it anyway! And if, after you have done what you felt was in alignment with your heart, and things still turn out to be a nightmare, don't worry! Remember – we aren't in the heat so that things will turn out perfect every time on the outside. We are in the heat to perfect our connection and perception of our inner Self so that we transform from amorphous carbon into diamonds!

Are we willing to simply dismiss the sticky situation as a mere thorn, or are we willing to see the situation as a door that will lead us to our own greatness? What have we drawn into our lives, and why? Why are we being tested, and how are we doing in the battle of life today?

Non-Dominant Hand Journaling opens your heart to the clarity and wisdom of your Higher Self, your inner knowing, and your inner voice. The practice of this technique cultivates your relationship with the inner wisdom you already have inside of you. Your Higher Self is with you always – even when you have shut it out and have forgotten about it. Remember, your Higher Self was with you in every moment of your life, and always will be. Use these Secrets as a medium of restoring your faith in your inner wisdom, of reconnecting with your inner truth, and of cultivating a relationship with your Higher Self. *This is the Real You.*

As your relationship with your Higher Self becomes stronger, the more you will trust your inner voice, and the more you will be in alignment with your soul. Soon you will find that inner voice becoming stronger, and you will no longer have to struggle to hear it – it will become *your* voice. As you start nurturing your Higher Self as the essence of who you are, you will soon realize that it is not a separate entity within yourself, *but it is you!*

Isn't that thrilling?
That Loving Wise Self is really YOU!

Close your eyes for a brief moment, and think about that: what it means to be fully identified with your Soul. Feel the joy welling up in your heart and the tears brimming in your eyes. Feel the continuous waves of peace coming over you and a quiet sense of contentment. Open your eyes, and look around you with the eyes of a Wise, Loving, and Compassionate Being. You are already that, you just have to improve your knowing!

As you practice these Secrets, the power of talking with your Higher Self will expand beyond the pages of your journal. You will find yourself turning to that inner voice for guidance as you drive on the freeway, pick an entrée at a restaurant, or close a business deal. As you become more attuned to your true Self, you will be less confused, irritable, or frustrated.

Cultivate that ability to follow your intuition, and suddenly, things will start making sense. Situations that seem to take over your life will soon shrink to a size you can handle.

Every time you worry, fear is tied up in knots in your stomach or it is spinning around in your mind so you can't sleep at night. Not too helpful, is it? Try writing down what you feel anxious about, or how you feel. Ask your Higher Self some questions, or just ask, "What's going on? What's the problem?"

Your Higher Self is really your intuition. It's your 6th sense of discrimination and insight. Just give your Higher Self ten minutes, and it will cut through the muddle and get down to the real stuff – what's your dharma, and how to follow your dharma no matter what.

If you have not done Secret #5 yet, now is your chance! It is time to know who you truly are! You are so great, you don't even know how great you are! You are the coolest, most amazing person you will ever meet. Put some quiet time into your relationship with yourself; it is the most important relationship you will ever have, and well worth the effort. Enjoy these moments with your journal to see your own beauty, your own light. Trust your own wisdom. Feel your own love within you. You have enough love and worthiness to fill up the universe a trillion times over, and dazzle the stars with your brilliance.

Don't wait for the perfect space, the perfect time, or the perfect person to follow your heart no matter what.

Now is your chance - Go for it! Live from your heart!

To be yourself in a world that is constantly trying to make you something else is the greatest accomplishment.

Ralph Waldo Emerson, Poet and Essayist

SECRET #6

Be Your Own Visionnaire

Imagine for a moment, that you got into a time machine, and it took you to 6th century Europe. If you were to tell people then, that the world is round, and you have pictures taken from outer space to prove it, they would laugh at you and call you crazy. They just won't believe you. They would have their own facts to prove to you that the world is flat! But no matter how many calculations they show you, or how much they express their deep convictions that the Earth is flat, you *know for a fact,* that the Earth is round! Nothing they say or do could make you believe otherwise, because to you, the Earth *is* round!

That is how real your purpose, your passion, and your dreams must be, that no matter what people say, you see it so clearly, that you *know* it is real.

Your dreams must be so real for you, that nobody can talk it out of you or laugh it out of you. It must be so real for you that all you have to do is make it a reality.

The reason that Disneyland came into being was that Walt Disney visualized it into reality. He saw it so vividly, down to every last detail, that nobody could come and shake the thought out of him. Nobody could tell him, "Oh this place doesn't exist!" because he had already seen it. He *knew* this fantasyland existed. It was as real for him in his mind, as it is for us today. In fact, it was so real, that he knew where every doorknob went, what it would look like, the color of the steps, and the carving of the wood. It was almost as if Disneyland already existed in the ether, and he had a special privilege to see it so that he could make it happen. So it is with your dreams. Your visions chose you. Be like Disney - own those glimpses of inspiration that have come to you. Those special goosebump moments came to you for a reason.

Revel in it! Be Your Own Visionnaire – see your vision, and make it happen!

What is your vision? What is the master plan? Those questions always seemed to elude me for some reason. I had lots of great ideas, many of which I did follow through on. The trouble was I could never grasp how all the puzzle pieces fit into the Big Picture. Some people know exactly what their vision is. Others know that they want to be an expert in their field, to buy a house, to get married, to have a family, or to travel two weeks of the year. There are the hi-falutin ones, who have all sorts of exotic visions which somehow fade away with time. And then there are the excited, passionate people like us, who are gung-ho, but not always too clear on our vision.

Out of convenience and my own personal reflection, I have come to the conclusion that you do not really need a life-long vision in order to fulfill your life's purpose.

Isn't that absolutely fantastic? If you have it, that is great. If you do not have it, then just know that if you were supposed to have a grand vision, it will reveal itself in its time. Right now, the only thing you need is to tap into the vision you have for yourself in this moment. This moment is all that really matters anyway, right?

You probably have heard of 'visualize your vision to reality,' or 'write what you want, and it will happen.' You might have tried it, and it did not always work. I know. I tried those techniques too, and they did not always work for me. That is, until I found the secret to making it happen a lot more. ***It is the magic of intention, drive, energy, and action.***

To make something happen or to create something, according to the Newtonian Law of Physics, requires work. To do work, you need to apply a force at a specific rate over a period of time. In order to apply a force, you need to input great amounts of energy in a certain direction.

Newton's Law is a universal physical law, which means that it applies to all of the physical universe. Makes sense, right? We are part of the physical universe, so Newton's Law applies to us as well.

Newton's Third Law states that for every force you exert in a certain direction, a force of equal intensity comes back to you from that direction. If you are having a hard time finding a job, and you start saying "Nobody's hiring," that is what will come back to you: no job. If you want to become a bestseller and you are taking your own sweet time to pick up your pen and write, your book will be taking its own sweet time to manifest. If, however, you zestfully and passionately start writing away, a few chapters every night until you are done, know that your bestseller is also passionately and zestfully racing towards you with the same energy and at the same rate you are moving towards it. It is the Law of Physics. It is the Law of how things work in the Universe. And it is the same Law of how things work for you.

Everything you are, everything your life is, and everything you have, you have created.

Give yourself a pat on the back! All the wonder and beauty, all the experiences you have drawn to your life and what you have become as a result, you have chosen. We create our lives – either consciously, or unconsciously.

Since you create your life intentionally or unconsciously, why not go all out and design the most grandiose life of your dreams? Dream big! Be Wacky! Be Crazy! Use your imagination! Write what you want your life to be...what *you* want to be! Give yourself half a chance; you will be surprised what your heart can see in store for you.

Begin by writing what a perfect day is for you. How do you get up in the morning...or where? What do you see outside your window? How do you feel? Describe the people you are with, what you are excited to eat, to wear, to do. What abilities do you have, how do people around you respond to you, to your passion, and to your life? Expand this to your life...what would be the perfect life for you? Describe your dream dharma, your dream home...or dream homes! It is there waiting for you.

Look at what you are and what you have already created in your life. See all the beauty that exists from moment to moment. If there is anything you do not want, change it! Just as you created it, you can create something else in its place. So choose what you want, and replace those old crusty fears and limiting wants with fresh budding beliefs and abundance. Anything you want... go right ahead and order it!

Abundant life is our birthright.

This universe is ours. Just as God created universes upon universes through His infinite imagination, so can we! He created us, and all the abilities He has, we have. When we still feel guilty for asking what we want, we are like a starving king who, sitting at his royal banquet that is overflowing with every delicacy possible, begs merely for a raisin.

What are you waiting for?
ASK! CREATE! MANIFEST!

In Secret #6, use your pen as a tool to allow your wants to flow through you and onto paper. This is a powerful experience in becoming conscious of what you are ready to create and manifest in your life at this time. A great perk for doing this creative process is that your wants become written and visible – two very important elements in making your visions a reality. As you allow yourself to write rapidly whatever comes to mind whenever you think of what your best year could be, or the best relationship, or your dream home…you are creating the blueprint for these things to manifest in your life. Just as it is hard to build a building without a plan, so it is hard to make your desires a reality when you do not have an idea of what you want. Makes sense, right?

So how do we create amazing things in our lives, even when we do not know what we want? How do we stay on purpose with our lives, without having a Master Plan?

Practice Secret #6! The process of writing what you want to create and manifest in your life, is called Creative Journaling.

Creative Journaling creates the living blueprints for your Master Plan to manifest into physical reality!

The act of writing what you want with passion and enthusiasm is a core ingredient to manifesting your dharma. Dream it. Write it. Bring it into the blueprint stage. You will see how much easier it will be to take action into manifesting your intentions. The old way of, "Know what you want, set goals, and bull-doze your way through to the end" never works. It is time to do something that *does* work, and fast.

SECRET #6: Be Your Own Visionnaire
Through Creative Journaling

1. Create your Journaling Ambience ~ set aside at least **15 minutes** for yourself, (no checking email, answering the phone, etc.) Light a few candles and incense.

2. Turn on your music player, and play Track 6, *Be Your Own Visionnaire SoundTrack,* from your Discover Your Dharma Soundtrack Album.

3. Open your journal to a new blank page, and write down the date, time, and your location.

4. Close your eyes for a moment, and picture yourself 10 years from now. What do you see? What do you look like? What are you wearing? Who are the people around you? Are you happy? Take a few moments to look into your eyes...how do you feel? If you want, ask your Future Self any question you would like. Allow it to respond. When it is time to leave your Future Self's presence, say, "Thank You." Now, open your eyes, and *super duper fast,* write whatever you want – any words of wisdom from your Future Self, or any notes on what you saw or felt. Was that a powerful experience?

5. Take a moment to breathe. Enjoy the sacredness of the moment. And embrace the wisdom and the knowing of your Future Self.

6. Now, turn to a new page. Write the date and time. Putting the Discover Your Dharma Soundtrack on Track 6 again, time yourself – give yourself 2 minutes to write… AS FAST AS POSSIBLE, anything and everything you want. Only rule: Start every sentence with the words *"I want…"* What if everything you wrote were to come true? Start writing and wanting like you never have before!

   Ok, one, two, three, GO!

   Example:
   (Writing super duper fast…)I want a back massage. I want a new comfy chair and a new desk. I want enlightenment. I want peace, patience, calmness, wisdom. I want to finish writing my book now! I want to be a bestseller, and to be spiritually, emotionally, and financially WEALTHY. I want to eat crepes and drink a pina colada right now! I want a new car, a big beautiful new home, and to enjoy the journey and get the most growth and joy and love out of life. I want to know and be with my soul mate. I want true happiness from the inside out. I want to be a kung fu master. I want to play tennis. I want to travel and to live all over the world. I want to go to Europe, Latin America, and Asia. I want to go to a warm tropical beach and bathe in the sea all day and all night. I want to play piano all night long. I want to speak French, Spanish, Hindi, Italian, and Portuguese fluently…

7. When you are done with the "I want…" frenzy, take 3 deep breaths, and relax. Breathe out your thoughts and your fears… Come to this exercise with an openness and excitement. You are co-creating your life with your Higher Self.

Imagine your life as a grand canvas. What would you paint? Who would you be? What life would you lead? See the images floating from your heart, surfacing as feelings and wants. Picture your life for a year, or picture yourself at the end of this year. Zestfully write at random what comes to mind. Use the same secret - start each sentence with the words, "I want….."

Example
I want to be happy. I want to be rich. I want a new car. I want a BMW Z4. I want a laptop to write my book anywhere with. I want to travel around the world. I want to go to Paris, London, the Caribbean, Brazil, Italy, and Greece this year. I want to make tons of new friends. I want to be on Oprah. I want to win a Nobel Prize, and an Oscar. I want every book I write to be a NYT bestseller. I want to be the star in a movie. I want to make my own CD's. I want to know My soul. I want peace in the world. I want a beautiful home on the beach. I want the most gorgeous garden. With lots of fruit trees and roses. And cool fountains and waterfalls…

8. After this process of writing what you want to create in your life, take a look at what you wrote. See what comes up for you when you look at your wants again…

- *Is it judgment?* These are feelings like, "I can't do this. I don't have the money. This is too good to ever happen to me." If you start breathing heavily, and you find yourself judging yourself or feeling guilty about outlandish dreams, this may be a good indicator that you're not ready to manifest this in your life right now. That's ok. You can choose to live your life as you do, maybe a little more consciously after this exercise. Or you can choose to introspect and practice some Socratic Journaling around why you feel you do not deserve to have what you want. *(See Secret #4)*

- *Is it anxiety?* If you have feelings like, "I know I could do this, I'm just scared of being bold enough to start my own business. What if I do fall in love with the right person? I don't know what would happen if I published a book..." these are good indicators of the fears that are still greater than your motivation to have what you want. You can use the technique of Introspective or Non-Dominant Hand Journaling (Secrets #2 and #5) to uncover limiting beliefs that keep you away from what is yours for the taking.

- *Is it excitement and elation?* If you have feelings like, "WOW! This is way awesome! I can't wait to do what I love, to travel, to buy my new home, to connect with people more, to be at peace, to have fun...!" then these are good indicators of your readiness and receptivity to the opportunities that will be presented to you. You are ready to do the next step – Step 9!

9. Notice how the Universe is supporting what you want for yourself. It is the power of setting an intention, tapping into the energy and drive, and knowing what right action to take. In recognizing and taking the opportunities as they come, you will begin making your blueprints a reality. Take a look at the pages you wrote your wants on. Notice what jumps out at you. Circle them, or make a mental note. This is a great way to tell which 'want' is ready to be manifested in your life at this time.

10. Now that you know how to do the Visionnaire Technique, let us take a look at what came out of your funnel in Secret #4, in order to take that Top 4 List to the next level. The following process will give you a clear action plan for your vision. Flip back through your journal, and pull out that 'Top 4' list.

Example from Secret #4, Step 10
Funnel Rankings outcome -

1. *Record music*
2. *Attend Script-Writing Program / Web-consulting*
3. *Live in Europe and travel/ photography when I travel*
4. *Live Shows with Band/ Make mini-music videos*

Let us start with the results from your 'Funnel Rankings':

Underline what you wrote for #1.

Let us say you wrote "To record music"

Now, take that underlined phrase, and use it to fill in the blanks to **Be Your Own Visionnaire:**

How will you choose to record music?

What kind of music?

When do you want to become a recorded artist?

What do you want to record?

Who would you like to record?

Where would you want to record – locally, abroad, through the label, privately, or do you want to create your own studio? Would you consider becoming a producer, recording other artists?

Now try it on your own – write each of the above questions in your journal, filling in the blanks for Item #1 from your 'Top 4' List.

After writing each question, write down your own answer. It shouldn't take very long to answer each prompt. In fact, do your best to write the first answer that comes to mind. Usually, these are the most intuitive responses.

Example in answering the questions yourself:
How will you choose to record music?
I will use Cubase software, my Audiogram MP3 converter, and my Yamaha XS7 keyboard to record all my music digitally. I can do it myself, and I don't need to buy studio time.

What kind of music?
I want to create my own music – all instrumental, inspiring, uplifting, cool, edgy, and new.

See? You get the gist. You can do the entire process for each item in your funnel ranking.

11. When you are done writing your quick responses, take a moment to look at what you wrote. What does the Big Picture look like, if you could dream about it a bit more?

Example
Our hearts are pounding and our ears are ringing as we get on stage at Madison Square Garden… the place is packed with millions of fans screaming to see us! I can't believe how things have turned out- way better than my wildest dreams! Bandmates are awesome, producer gets our vision, manager is ten steps ahead, and our label is plugging us everywhere. It's been a wild ride – this is our 100th show – we've just traveled to 15 countries, and had the most memorable international tour! We've been nominated for several Grammy awards, and our music is an Oscar-winning soundtrack for a movie score! Life couldn't be better! Feels great to be home again… looking forward to getting back in the studio and recording the next album. I want to be a producer too, and start my own independent label. It feels so awesome to make other people's dreams come true too!

There is no holding back! Let loose, and write with unprecedented speed, any images that come to mind, sounds, feelings, events, or things you can see as turning points. Write what would be the pinnacle of success for you. Use words to paint your vision by creating the big picture. How is it going to be? What is it going to look like? How is it going to feel? What would it mean to you? How will it change your life? What is the legacy you will leave behind? How will you react when this happens? Are you jumping for joy? Feel the high energy surging through you and infuse your vision with it! Come on, it is time to Be Your Own Visionnaire!

12. When 10 minutes are up and you are all done, SLAM YOUR JOURNAL SHUT, AND DECLARE LOUDLY TO THE UNIVERSE, "I AM A VISIONNAIRE!"

In addition to discovering your dharma, this creative process is especially good at New Year's time, on your birthday, getting into a relationship or getting out of one, or any other major life transition. Be your own Visionnaire – see your vision, and make it happen in your own way!

Immerse yourself in this powerful creative process as you co-create your path, making these blueprints come into being, and beckoning them into the present.

When you live passionately and on purpose, you not only get what you want, but also more than you could possibly contain!

Why is that? In E.V. Ingraham's **Wells of Abundance**, he comments on the power of this creative process. He remarks, "The faithful practice of the preceding steps should, ere now, have brought you into perfect accord with this process. Your supply should spring forth speedily and abundantly." According to the Law of Abundance, your abundance moves eternally and infinitely. Just as water piles up behind a dam, your abundance is stored up for you. This is the reason you feel pressure to manifest your goals and wants. You think the pressure is the weight or oppression of lack, but it isn't. As Ingraham emphasizes, it is actually the pressure of your Universal bank account, the unused resource of your nature that is crowding itself upon you. If you have not used much, it is not lost. It is still yours, rushing you down wherever you go.

As Emerson wrote so eloquently:

Hast not thy share?
Lo, it rushes thee to meet.
All that nature made thine own,
Floating in air or pent in stone,
Shall rive the hills and swim the sea
And, like thy shadow follow thee.

Isn't that wonderful? Your abundance has your name on it, *rushing* to meet you! ARE YOU EXCITED YET? I am!

Now that you have mastered this Sixth Secret, you are ready to use the upcoming Secrets to make your Big Picture a Reality! Great Job! It is time to get rolling and live joyously!

Every moment of your life your good is seeking you out!

All things you need for your progress are moving toward you. Trust and know with certainty that all your wants are waiting for you. If you do not use it or take it, it is still there waiting for you. Have no doubt about it! Whatever you can see and believe, is already yours! See it, feel it, and make it happen!

There is only one question: when will you choose to receive it?

If one advances confidently in the direction of one's dreams, and endeavors to live the life which one has imagined, one will meet with a success unexpected in common hours.

Henry David Thoreau, Journaler, Author & Philosopher

SECRET #7

Fuel Your Mission with Volition

In his 1962 speech delivered at Rice University in Houston, Texas, President John F. Kennedy declared America's commitment to go to the moon before the end of that decade. At the time, scientists did not think they could accomplish this in forty years, but the President was undeterred in his resolve. He had a vision, and declared it to the whole world that day:

"We choose to go to the moon! We choose to go to the moon in this decade and do the other things, not because they are easy, but because they are hard, because that goal will serve to organize and measure the best of our energies and skills, because that challenge is one that we are willing to accept, one we are unwilling to postpone, and one which we intend to win."

In less than a decade, against all odds, and to the amazement of the whole world, President Kennedy's declaration had come true. On July 20, 1969, NASA's astronauts became the first to walk on the moon.

What a testament to the power of intention, the power of commitment, and the power of declaration! Imagine if we did that in our own lives. What would it look like? What would it feel like to energize your vision into your Life Mission? Are you shooting for the moon? And if not, why not?

It is hard to keep the vision alive every day. Or even a couple hours from now! Wherever you direct your attention, there your energy goes. How do you 'stay on track' when you believe that you are 'sidetracked'? How do you keep your vision going, when you feel that you have forgotten all about it?

I will share with you **Secret # 7: Fuel Your Mission with Volition.** Are you ready for the Secret?

> **Write your way out of inaction by affirming what you want, as if you already have it!**

The power of Affirmative Journaling lies in the *act* of writing, the act of affirming, and the act of pouring energy and redirecting your thoughts on what you want. Especially when you feel down, or you feel you are the only one having to fight an uphill battle, this Secret is a lifesaver.

The unique feature of this energizing technique is that you can practice it all the time. Over the past ten years, I have used this technique during those times that I felt I was losing the vision the most. Like writing this book, for example. I finished it in two weeks, and then I dilly-dallied until so much time passed by, I forgot to infuse it with enthusiasm, spirit, and focus, and just get it published. I had gotten so caught up with working, teaching, and traveling, that before I knew it, months had passed by. People would ask me, "So, how's the book? Is it done yet?" And I would remember – oh yeah, my book! Time to get cracking! But how? What do you do when nobody supports you out there, and you have to get up and keep on keeping on?

I would come to the 200-page file of my book, and make notes of what to remember to do, and then hop on the internet and check my email…and you know the rest, that was the end of working on my book for the day! Unlike pressure and deadlines that come from the outside, I did not have the same pressure to finish my book. There was no deadline except for the one I gave myself, and there was no immediate consequence for not sticking to it.

It finally came to a point where I got used to not finishing my book. It was the never-ending project. That is, until it was four months after the date it should have been published. That was when I hit a wall. The only thing that saved me was this Secret I am about to share with you.

We can energize our vision, and manifest our Life Mission by using the same technique President Kennedy used in 1962 to accomplish the Mission to the Moon.

I am sure you have probably tried those old affirmation tricks – write your goals in present tense with a blue pen on a blue index card, and repeat it over and over. I have done it too. I went to the store, bought my blue index cards, came home, and got a big blue marker. I was ready to affirm! I wrote my affirmation down: "I am a millionaire!" I looked in the mirror and affirmed it for a few minutes. Then I closed my eyes, and visualized what it would feel like to have a million dollars. After pumping myself up, I turned around, went into the kitchen to find something to eat, and for the next 23 hours and 57 minutes of the day, I kept thinking, *"Yeah right, I'm not a millionaire. I don't have enough money to do that. I need to get a better job."* What was I unconsciously affirming? That I am not a millionaire! Whatever thoughts and beliefs we cultivate in our minds, that reality is what we create. No matter what we write in blue ink for three minutes, our reality is what we think.

Affirmation is something we all do, unconsciously or consciously. It is so powerful we do not even realize that we do it 24 hours a day, 7 days a week. Everything we are now, we have affirmed ourselves into being. We affirm we are rich; we affirm we are poor. We affirm everybody loves us; we affirm nobody loves us. We affirm we are awesome, magnificent, and fantastic; we affirm we are poor unfortunate failures. Whatever we say comes to pass. It is the power of subconscious thought; it is the power of words.

Write down those same words you say all the time, and you will concretize the power of their sound vibrations into the physical reality of the written word.

Ever notice the strains of songs that get stuck in your head? The singer repeats the chorus over and over and over again, until you hear it in your head too... hours, days, and weeks later. That is the simple power of affirmation. So, how do we use affirmation to put our volition into gear? How do we use it to accomplish our mission?

> **It is the positive repetition and energizing of a thought that brings about belief, creating opportunities for the thought or object of attraction to become a physical reality. This is known as the Affirmation Principle.**

That is really the fundamental premise for Secret #7. In consciously applying this Principle to your approach to Affirmative Journaling, you can see that this is not just a little affirmation technique, to waste your time writing things that are not real for you. This Secret is the conscious power of writing, engaging the power of your mind and the vibratory responses of the physical Universe to manifest those thought vibrations you are putting on paper.

Invoke the power of this Seventh Secret, and put your mind and heart into it. The distractions and delusion of this world are very strong. It is very rare that one can sustain focus, passion, and purpose, without having doubts, or feeling off-track. When we hit a low point, it is important to have a trusty reliable tool, like this Secret, to withstand the winds as they come to test us.

We get stuck in the idea that just by affirming what we want, we will instantly get it. And then when we do not instantly get what we want, we give up. What we do not realize is that we ARE getting what we affirmed! Is it any wonder that we get what we do not want? It is what we affirmed the most!

When you make an affirmation, and write it down repeatedly with fervor and excitement, you instantly begin the creation of what you want. Isn't that exciting? Just by writing it down, just by affirming what you want, you are activating the process of going from blueprints to physical manifestation. The Secret is: you have to be open. You have to be aware of the process.

Opportunities do not always come with bold letters or the limitations you may put on them. Let us say you are looking for a position as a teacher. You do the affirmation formula, and you start looking online to see if there are any schools hiring. While you are fixing up your resume, you are invited to go to a beach party. Your intuition tells you to go to the party. But your mind says you should really stay home, fix your resume, and look for a job. You decide to go to the party, and you unexpectedly meet someone's friend who is a principal for a school, and he offers you a job. If you had not gone to the party, you might not have met him. Haven't you had an experience like that before? Sometimes the opportunity to get what we want may come in the most innocuous ways; sometimes the opportunities are direct. You are the only one who will know when it is your chance, and when it is not.

In order to create powerful intuitive affirmations, you have to come from a calmer, deeper place within yourself.

Calmness is the doorway to clarity.

When you are attuned to your Higher Self, your self-affirmations are in alignment with your purpose. You will know what to do next, seizing the opportunities that present themselves so that you can manifest what you need, when you need it.

If you know how to meditate, practice 5-10 minutes of meditation before and after Affirmative Journaling to infuse more power and energy into your affirmations. It will increase the intensity and the timing in which your affirmation becomes a reality. Meditation will also help you move from confusion or ego-blockages to awareness and clarity, thus making your affirmations more likely to come true.

Scientists have proven that the subconscious mind has no discrimination – it believes and takes as truth everything it is told. Feed your subconscious mind with all the things you want to be in reality, and give yourself a chance to write your own destiny!

That is exactly what I did when I started on the path of consciously co-creating my life mission. Re-evaluating as I went, I practiced this Seventh Secret like crazy. Once I realized the deeper powers of affirmation, and the secret to make it work for me, I discovered the Affirmation Formula.

I am extremely passionate about this Formula, because I believe it will be the key to you living your Life Mission with ease, and to fulfilling your vision when you leave this Discover Your Dharma Intensive, and go out into the world. It may seem that the world is full of distractions, constantly bombarding you to take you away from your Goal. How do you keep your torch burning bright when you feel you have no support? While you are encouraged to participate in our empowering programs and our Make Your Vision Happen Teams to keep you on track with living your dharma, the Affirmation Formula is the key to activating your own inner support system. With this powerful tool, you can re-energize your vision anytime you want.

Remember John F. Kennedy's Mission to the Moon? Would you like to know the key ingredients that got NASA on the Moon in such a short time?

The Affirmation Principles in action!

The Affirmation Formula:

KNOW what your mission is, claim it, and constantly re-energize it with high energy both mentally and physically.

DECLARE what you want, or intend to do, with unshakable force, so you invoke the power of your purpose.

COMMIT and get firm on the inside, so when you meet conflicts or challenges on the outside, you just shake them off and step up to the plate.

ACT in congruence and in pursuit of your mission with focus and conviction.

Now that you know the Formula, how do you do it? Where do you start? Let us look at what we have so far from the previous Secrets:

1. You know what you want to do.
   (Secret #2: Moment of Truth)
2. You have the 'big picture' in mind.
   (Secret #6: Be Your Own Visionnaire)

Let us say you start out excited, on purpose, and things are falling into place. Somehow, without trying too hard, you see the opportunity, and hop on it. One thing leads to another, and soon, you find yourself a couple months down the road, invested in your vision. But as new priorities come up, which they inevitably will, your energies shift, your excitement begins to fade, and you get distracted and occupied in other directions. One morning you will wake up, you know what you have to do, but you just don't feel like it. What do you do when you do not feel like pursuing your dreams? Have you ever felt this way? You are going great, on track, following through, and then, as the weeks go by, you start getting distracted, off course, and lose momentum. All this passion stuff goes to the ditches. Now what? I know it is just not possible to be passionate 100% of the time, morning, noon, and night, right? It is normal to get bogged down and lose the vision sometimes. What do you do then?

You practice Secret #7 - FAST!

Affirm what you *do* want in your life, what you want to achieve, what you want to attract, and how you want to feel! You know the saying, "You've got to believe in order to make it happen." What if you don't believe, yet? The good news is: you don't have to believe *at first,* in order to make things happen for you!

Affirmative journaling *creates belief!*

The more you are affirming, the more you are attracting and seeing the opportunities as they present themselves, and so automatically, you believe! What you believe, is your reality. As you manifest what you want, you are reinforcing the beliefs you put out into the universe. As a Talmudic saying goes,"We do not see things as they are; we see things as we are."

You do not have to believe right now that you are a legendary interior-decorator or a world-renowned artist. Just practice affirming that you are one, and the affirmation process will take care of the belief part. Remember, everything in this universe begins with thought, including the next step for you. In affirming the thought or idea you would like to manifest, you are actually energizing and activating that thought so you believe it is true.

When you believe, and when you focus on what you want, you begin attracting opportunities to yourself so you can make your vision a reality. It is very important to understand this principle of affirmation. I want you to put your pen down for a second and take a deep breath. Declare to the Universe "I am paying attention!" Snap your fingers to let the Universe know you are ready for what you are affirming.

When we practice the science of affirmation, and the Affirmation Formula, we are instantaneously putting the Affirmation Principle into effect in our lives. That is how powerful it is. Use it often, and with care!

Are you ready for this powerful Secret?

Secret #7: Fuel Your Mission with Volition
Through The 7-Step Affirmative Journaling Process

1. Create your Journaling Ambience ~ set aside at least **15 minutes** for yourself, (no checking email, answering the phone, etc.) Light a few candles and incense.

2. Turn on your music player, and play Track 7, *Fuel your Mission With Volition SoundTrack,* from your Discover Your Dharma Soundtrack Album.

3. Open your journal to a new page. Write the date, time, and your location.

4. Begin with a thought, original want, or desire. Affirm that thought by writing it over and over in your journal.

   EXAMPLE of Affirmative Journaling:
   [Let's say you're in the music industry, you could write…] *I'm a Grammy Winner! I'm a Grammy Winner! I'm a Grammy Winner! I'm a Grammy Winner! I'm a Grammy Winner! I'm a Grammy Winner! I'm a Grammy Winner! I'm*

a Grammy Winner! I'm a Grammy Winner! I'm a Grammy Winner! I'm a Grammy Winner! I'm a Grammy Winner! I'm a Grammy Winner! I'm a Grammy Winner! That's my hit song! I love my fans! That's my hit song! I love my fans! That's my hit song! I love my fans! That's my hit song! I love my fans! That's my hit song! I love my fans! That's my hit song! I love my fans! That's my hit song! I love my fans! That's my hit song! I love my fans!
THANK YOU! THANK YOU! THANK YOU!!!!

5. Energize that thought by visualizing it as if it were real in your mind's eye. Look at yourself, smiling, accomplished, content, exuberant, in the place where you want to be, doing what you love, being with the people you want to be with, and giving what you have to give.

6. Look at what you have written, and repeat it again and again!
   VOICE IT!
   SAY IT ALOUD WITH PASSION!
   SAY IT WITH CONVICTION!
   SAY IT WITH VOLITION!
   SAY IT WITH EVERY FIBER OF YOUR BEING!
   SAY IT LIKE YOU WANT IT!
   Create the belief that it IS possible to become a reality!

7. You can continue the Affirmative Journaling process, by following the techniques outlined in the upcoming pages, under the heading ***5 Powerful Ways of Affirmative Journaling.***

8. When the music track is over, SLAM YOUR JOURNAL SHUT, AND SAY "YES! I FUEL MY MISSION WITH VOLITION!" Then close your eyes, and softly whisper your affirmation, until you begin to repeat it over and

over in your mind. Continue to practice it as soon as you wake up in the morning, and before you go to bed.

Take *action* as every opportunity presents itself. Say 'YES!' to invitations or information the Universe delivers to you. Be open and amazed at how much the Universe bends to give you what you ask for! That's Volition!

Then say it aloud with all the energy of your body, and let the words sink into your being. Affirm it everywhere in your life – talk about it, live it, and be it. It takes 5 minutes to affirm, and it is like opening a portal to your inner Genie, where you have infinite wishes to be fulfilled just by rubbing the lamp of affirmation. Go for it! Make what you want a reality! If you have not done it yet – what are you waiting for? The clock is ticking, and whatever you can write and affirm, is yours!

The Art of Affirmative Journaling

What does it mean to affirm? According to the Merriam Webster Dictionary, the definitions of *affirm* and *affirmation* are:

affirm (verb)
1: a. to validate, confirm. b: to state positively
2: to assert (as a judgment or decree) as valid or confirmed
3: to express dedication to

affirmation (noun)
the act of affirming or asserting or stating something

The magic of this technique is that once you continuously write what you want with passion and conviction, it will strengthen your ability to manifest that thought into physical reality. Just like prayers, the answers may come at different times, different ways, or different forms, but the more specific and focused you are, the more likely it will be to come true.

The easiest way to do this technique is to start writing down things you want. Affirmations come in shiploads...the more you write, the more there is to write! If there is something you really really want, write it down over and over and over. Say it aloud and repeat it mentally while you write. There is a power that activates the affirmation when you:

1. *Say it aloud (the vibratory power of speaking),*
2. *Write it down (the visible and tangible power of writing), and*
3. *Repeat it mentally (the creative power of the mind.)*

This type of journaling is very flexible. It can be mixed into other journaling techniques, or you can set aside a few minutes and a fresh new page just for this. Either way, the process is the same, and it is just as effective and powerful.

The 5 Powerful Techniques to Practice Affirmative Journaling

I. Affirm in the *Present Tense*

Write in the present tense what you want to get or what you want to be. If you want to be an Olympic Gold Medalist, you can write: "I am an Olympian! I am a Gold Medalist! I am on that podium waving my country's flag!"

Write as if you already have what you want for yourself in the future.

If you want to be patient, you can write: "I am so patient. I am calm, collected, and patient." Writing in the present tense is affirming that you already possess the thing or quality you want. Remember, the subconscious mind has no discretion. If you say you have it, your mind thinks you have it, and so it takes it as truth that you already have that Gold Medal. There is a spot on that Olympic team, or the perfect house out there for you, waiting for you to ask for it. In affirming in the present tense, your mind believes you have it already, and it goes about creating opportunities to 'manifest' your desire into reality.

II. Affirm by writing *"I want..."*

Sometimes, the things I really want seem so far away that I want to make them real to me so that I can manifest them in my life. So I go into an *"I want...."* frenzy to stir up the energy and get it flowing again. For this one, you just put pen to paper, and time yourself for 5 minutes. Without stopping, write as fast as possible, starting each sentence with the words: *"I want..."* and let your inner 'want machine' fill in the blanks.

Example:

"I want this book done. I want it published. I want it edited. I want millions of people reading it...."

You can keep going in related categories or on a tangent of other things you want - whatever you feel called to do. The point is to crank up the inner 'want machine'. If you can't think of anything else to write before the 5 minutes are up, then just re-write what you wrote over and over again until the time is up. The key is to keep writing, and to affirm what you want by writing it down with excitement and speed!

III. Affirm by writing *"I have..."*

What if you feel like you haven't gotten the things you really want? Then you may want to practice this kind of affirmative journaling by starting each sentence with the words, *'I have..."* You may think, "Isn't this like lying to yourself? You're saying you have things when you don't? What's the point of that?"

Remember, your subconscious mind cannot tell the difference between what is real and what is not real. It thinks everything that it conceives, is real. Your brain responds to the real and the unreal in the exact same way. If you affirm what you *would like to have as if you already have it,* your brain will think that you do! When your brain and subconscious mind think you already have what you want, you will find yourself having an easier time acquiring/fulfilling your vision. Why? Because, to your mind, it is now possible!

Here is an example of this kind of affirmative writing, starting each sentence with the words, *I have…:*

I have a beautiful home overlooking the ocean. I can smell the ocean. I have a most wonderful garden. I have …"

IV. Write "Thank You" for What you *Want*

This type of affirmative journaling is my favorite. It is the easiest and the most powerful, at least for me. Even though you have not received what you want yet, you are giving thanks for your desires being fulfilled.

When we say 'Thank You,' we usually say that *after* we have received something. It is how we express our gratitude. In the act of thanking the Universe for what you want, you are not asking for what you could have, but saying 'Thank You' for what you have received – again a feeling of something after it has passed. Your mind knows that feeling, so it thinks you have already gotten what you have asked for, and will go about ensuring that what you want is a part of your reality.

Let us say you really want a new Yamaha motorcycle. Instead of writing, *"I want a Yamaha motorcycle,"* you can write, *"Thank You for my new AWESOME Yamaha motorcycle!"* Your mind – and the Universe – get the message that you are ecstatic and grateful for that Yamaha motorcycle and so opportunities are created to ensure that you are the Owner of a new Yamaha Motorcycle!

Want to give it a shot?

1. Put on Track 1 of the Discover Your Dharma Soundtrack.
2. Put pen to paper for **five minutes** or the length of one music track. When the track is over, you can stop journaling.

3. Begin writing as fast as possible, starting each sentence with "Thanks for ______." Fill in the blank with something you want to acquire, something you want to happen, or who you want to be in the future. Keep writing 'Thanks' for these wants until time is up. See example below.
4. When time is up, finish writing your last sentence. Then SLAM YOUR JOURNAL SHUT and say "THANK YOU FOR EVERYTHING!"

Here's an example where I thank the Universe for things I have not gotten yet:

Thank you for my new haircut! I absolutely love it! Thanks for my new dress! Thanks for the matching shoes! Thanks for my book getting published! Thanks for getting straight A's. Thanks for my new place! Thanks for my car – I love driving it on the freeway… and parking it. Yeah…that's my car! Thanks! Thanks for the most relaxing, enjoyable time with my friends and family in Hawaii. Thanks for perfect weather, and getting the villa on the oceanfront. Thanks for the spectacular view, and cool breezes in the evenings. Thanks for the beautiful sunsets, and a beautiful time with each other…

Gratitude Affirmative Journaling creates a feeling of worthiness and receptivity for what we want. Sometimes, we are so attached to the 'wanting' that we get used to the idea that it is always off in the distance, somewhere in the future – not really ever in the present. If we don't get that home, that job, or that relationship we want, we think it's not possible right now. But, in reality, it is because *we are not ready for it right now.*

It might be useful to reflect on why we don't have what we want now. Is it because now isn't the time? Or could it be that we are afraid? We may think, "If I knew my life's purpose, I wouldn't have the excuse of skylarking on the weekends with my friends, or being spontaneous and travel to another country for a few months. What if I don't want to be focused and passionate and on track every morning? What if I need to hide behind my excuses and lack of direction? What if I want to work hard but don't want to be attached to the results? Would my friends think I'm stuck up if I were to drive a Ferrari now? Or be a millionaire now? If I were to find my 'soulmate' now, would that mean I'd have to be tied down, and won't get to travel, or be as independent as I am now?"

It is good to be honest with yourself and to be aware of where you are and what is going on inside of you. You can affirm from now until doomsday that you want to find your soulmate, but if you feel that it might hamper your freedom and your need to explore, then either the affirmation won't work, or you will always sabotage what you attract in your life. As a result, the persons you attract are NOT your 'soulmate' type. And the same goes for your dharma, fulfilling your vision, buying a new house, or anything else you may want for that matter.

Want to hear the good news? The good news is no matter if you have fears or deep-rooted self-sabotaging bad habits, this Gratitude Affirmative Journaling technique is unparalleled in its power to move mountains and increase your receptivity to that which you truly desire for yourself. Isn't that liberating?

If you keep on saying thanks for what you want – whether it is a virtue, a feeling, or something in your life – *just the process of doing this technique* will overcome those self-sabotaging grooves in your brain, and create new grooves for getting what you want.

That is the real power of this type of declaration. It is physically changing the neural wiring in your brain, while connecting it to a *feeling* of being grateful and already having what you want! How amazing is that? It is even more amazing when you try it, and see how it works before your own eyes!

V. Affirm by Repetition

The most powerful way to affirm is to repeat your affirmation over and over and over. This age-old technique works on your subconscious, conscious, and superconscious minds, and has proven its power the world over, from the spiritual mantras of ancient civilizations to the Nike™ slogan *"Just do it."*

Repetition brands the words into your subconscious mind so that it is an imprinted image in your mind's eye. The vibratory and visual repetition of your affirmation becomes a reality in your mind, making it easier to become manifested in your life. The more you affirm that you are patient, the more your mind focuses on how patient you are. As a result, you increasingly notice the times you do practice patience. Soon, you only see when you are patient, and over time, you are much more patient because now, you believe you are! The same thing goes for impatience, unfortunately! The more you keep saying, "Gosh, I don't have time! I have no patience for this!" the more you are affirming that you are impatient. Soon, you will start seeing how impatient you are on the freeway, waiting in line at the grocery store, or getting things done at work. Over time, you actually do become a frustrated impatient person.

Be wise in choosing your affirmations, and what you say to yourself repeatedly.

Why keep on repeating to ourselves, "Geez, I'm such a klutz." Or, "I'm not such a great writer. I can't write a book..." when we could be affirming, "Wow, I'm so awesome! I'm such a great writer! My book is the best!" If what you think becomes your reality, why not start saying and writing what you want now?

The Affirmation Formula in Action

How do you put your Mission into Motion? Once you ignite your rocket, it requires an abundant amount of fuel in order to break out of the stratosphere and stay on course. Missions do not stay on course automatically; they need your utmost *focus, energy, intention,* and *commitment.*

Remember President Kennedy's declaration, and the Mission to the Moon? Remember the Affirmation Formula? Here it is again:

The Affirmation Formula

KNOW what your mission is, claim it, and constantly re-energize it with high energy both mentally and physically.

DECLARE what you want, or intend to do, with unshakable force, so you invoke the power of your purpose.

COMMIT and get firm on the inside, so when you meet conflicts or challenges on the outside, you just shake them off and step up to the plate.

ACT in congruence and in pursuit of your mission with intention and with purpose.

In the first four Secrets, we discovered the first part – KNOW your mission. In this Seventh Secret, we are doing the second part of that formula: DECLARE what you want. Write over and over what you want as if you already have it. Just the *process* of practicing this Seventh Secret makes the magic formula come to life. You don't have to know how your vision is going to happen. You just have to put energy and excitement into the next step before you. Then you have to be COMMITTED to your vision by putting the principle of commitment from Secret #4 into practice. Finally, take ACTION. Success rewards action. When you are afraid, when you feel confused, when you feel lost, or when you feel overwhelmed – take action! In doing something, you begin to apply energy in a certain direction. Remember Newton's Third Law of Physics? The more fervent you are moving towards your Goal, the faster it is moving towards you! That is all you ever have to do!

FUEL YOUR MISSION WITH VOLITION!

Affirmation:

I FUEL MY MISSION WITH VOLITION!
I AM POWERFUL BEYOND MEASURE!
I AM THE MASTER OF MY DESTINY!

While small-minded men cry 'impossible', the pathfinders of the world calmly pursue their goals and demonstrate that the impossible was, instead, inevitable.

Paramahansa Yogananda, yogi and spiritual world teacher

SECRET #8

Do Your Dailies!

Inspired by the Socratic philosophy that an 'unexamined life is not worth living,' Thoreau never strayed from the close lens of his journal. One of the greatest philosophers, political-activists, and writers of all time, Henry David Thoreau began journaling as a young Harvard student in 1837, and never missed a day until the end of his life in 1858. With great rigor, honesty, and humor, Thoreau was a master at examining his thoughts, his feelings, his beliefs, and his relation to the observable world around him.

A natural scientist and historian, Thoreau delighted in conducting 'self-experiments.' As an experiment of his introspective philosophy, Thoreau moved into a small cabin on Walden Pond, which was only a mile from his home. Thoreau lived in solitude to observe himself, and the response of society to his actions. In the two years, two months, and two days that he lived at Walden, he wrote profusely. Thoreau filled pages upon pages in his journals of his thoughts, his observations of nature, his convictions, and his philosophical musings of life, virtue, and nature. More than a century later, these journals stand as a powerful testimony to Secret #8: Do Your Dailies. Why? Long after his death, Thoreau's journals were considered a collective literary classic, a political text on civil disobedience, and a work of scientific contribution. Thoreau's transformation happened in the writing with his journals, and his life is an inspiration to anyone who uses the journal as a tool to discover his own dharma.

The running thread of Thoreau's journals, illustrate the power of 'daily journaling.' In reflecting on the events and feelings he experienced throughout the day, Thoreau explored his thoughts, experiences, and observations. Trusting in the beauty of Nature and the workings of the Universe, Thoreau sought the answers of life drawn from inspiration he garnered in the woods around him. From looking at beavers making their homes, to birds singing in the trees, Thoreau developed the art of observation with attunement and attentiveness. With this same curiosity, non-judgmentalism, and wonder, Thoreau approached his own life. He grew deeper in his personal convictions and beliefs, as he strengthened his relationship with his inner voice via his journal. The more he was in contact with his heart's wisdom, the less he was concerned with what people said about his 'wanderings' and 'living in the woods.' With a wisdom and a deep acumen well beyond his time, Thoreau unlocked the Eighth Secret for us.

Throughout history, the lives of men and women have told countless stories of tragedy and triumph in order to answer a fundamental question of the human existence: why are we here, and how do we fulfill our purpose? We can learn a lot from the lives of others. In the quiet but diligent practice of daily journaling, the answer emerges – not as words on paper, but in our own transformation and enlightenment.

What you become as a result of daily celebration and introspection is the measure of your progress, your thought patterns, and your potential.

Thoreau's rigorous practice of daily journaling provided the limitless laboratory in which he was able to experience transformation. The journal, in and of itself, does not hold the answers we seek.

We are the ones who are writing, and it is in the process of writing our thoughts, feelings, and experiences of the day, that *we enlighten ourselves.*

How do we look at the triumphs in our own lives? How do we measure our growth, our thought patterns, and our progress? It is hard to recall all of the events from the past years, or even last week!

That is the power of daily journaling – to record, to notice, and to consciously experience your growth on a deeper level.

When you look back at your journals over the years, you will be able to see the thinking patterns and behaviors you had at that time, the patterns you still have now, and the patterns you have changed since then. You will also be able to see why you made certain choices then, and why you make those same choices now. We often make choices unconsciously for our lives, without understanding why we do what we do. For most of us, our default mode justifies our dead-end habitual patterns of thinking. After all of these years, do you still feel lonely, abandoned, worthless, or not good enough? And do those feelings occur no matter what you do, what you look like, or who you are with?

In experimental science, the **observer effect** occurs when the act of observing changes the phenomenon being observed. This effect was derived from an experiment that was designed to 'see' an electron. To do this, a photon (a massless elementary particle that carries energy) must interact with the electron by transferring energy, and thus change the path of the electron. Introspection is actively looking within with the intention of observation and transformation. Scientifically, the observer does impact the observed. It is *because* the observer is present, the observed is affected. To be present with your inner self and your inner life, and to see that connection with your outer self and your outer life, is to influence your life experience for the better, especially if your True Nature is what you seek! The traditional art of keeping a diary was more or less a record-keeping activity. In the art of daily journaling – journaling *about* your day – the act of journaling contributes to the transformation that occurred in the experiences you had that day. This technique is an act that creates awareness, a tool that contributes to deeper understanding, and is also a testimonial to who you are in this moment, and what you have been through today.

The Eighth Secret - the daily exploration of your life - is part of the creative process. Sounds a bit odd? Think about it: you can create and recreate, correct and shift gears in your life, by assessing what is happening on the inside and the outside. While our outer life seems to be glamorous, colorful, demanding, and ever-prodding, our inner life may be almost nonexistent. Conversely, our outer life may seem like it is doomed, hellish, and a nightmare, while on the inside, we are transforming enormously at a terrific rate. How do we know what is really happening with us, if we never took a moment to look closer? This Eighth Secret provides us the opportunity to truly live fully. What does that mean? It means to embrace all of the aspects of life we are experiencing, and to open our eyes to the creative power of choice every single moment. If we want to go to Los Angeles, and we just head out our door and start walking, without looking at the road signs, the landmarks, or the scenery around us, we may end up at the North Pole for all we know!

> **Daily Journaling allows you to get a good look at those signs that remind you where you are going, to let you know when you are on track, and to fully experience the journey.**

Are we living just to take up space, to see if we qualify to live another day? Or are we living life that we may get something out of it, that we *become* something greater because of it? The more we journal about our feelings and experiences, the more we understand why we are having these experiences. And the more understanding we have about what is going on in our lives, the more we understand, accept, and love our *Selves*. That is the essence of the Eighth Secret.

I did not realize it at the time, but I was first introduced to the Eighth Secret when I was fourteen years old. Out on a debate tournament at Harvard University, my friends and I were waiting well beyond our bedtime, to compete. Hungry, sleepy, and anxious, my friend's head was reeling.

Holding her head in her hands, she exclaimed,

"Gosh, I have such a terrible headache!"

I don't know what came over me, but I responded consolingly, "Tell it to go away!"

She looked at me quizzically. "Huh?"

"Yes, just tell your headache to go away. Just visualize it melting away, and try to feel your head as if it were normal again."

Up for the challenge, she tried it. And it worked! Not only then, but for the two years after that, at countless tournaments and before hundreds of exams, we commanded our nerves and headaches to go away. While part of the lesson was the power of words, the other part was: if we could tell our troubles to go away, that means we had, at one point, attracted our troubles to us in the first place! That was when I realized that really and truly, nothing *happens to us.* We create our happiness and our misery, our triumphs and our troubles. We have certain experiences so that we could learn the lessons we need to learn. But, more often than not, we suffer greatly because we do not examine our beliefs, and we tend to think things *have* to be a certain way, when they do not really need to be! We assumed headaches just 'happen', and the only way to cure it was to eat, sleep, and take some aspirin. By noticing that we got headaches whenever we were angry or anxious, we realized that we were the creators of our headaches. In fact, we did not *have* to suffer in the first place!

We have the power to create our experiences, and to control our reactions and responses.

Observing patterns that seem to 'happen' to us, we can explore why we attract these positive and negative experiences in our lives. Armed with this information we are empowered to create transformation in our lives from moment to moment. Throughout high school, I was always nauseous before my speeches. In acknowledging this, I hoped that one day, I would not be nauseous at all. Ten years later, after practicing Secret #7 and the Affirmative Journaling Technique, in conjunction with this Secret #8, I was able to cure myself of the pre-speech nausea. Pretty powerful stuff!

How do we stay on track with ourselves, and our dharma? You know the answer – Secret #8, of course!

Our purpose is to discover who we are *in the process* of accomplishing things.

Of all the techniques you do, you will find Daily Journaling to be a powerful process in physically and internally cultivating a conscious, authentic lifestyle. By being aware of what you are truly feeling, whether you expressed it to someone today or not, you allow yourself to rise to the challenge of living authentically. This is a huge step in increasing self-awareness. Soon you will notice how well you express yourself, or how well you listen and honor your feelings. You will also begin to see when you are in alignment with your heart, and when you are out of sync. As you develop the art of honestly writing your daily experiences, you will start bringing this authenticity into your relationship with yourself. It is the most incredible feeling to be truly honest. This is what living authentically means - living by your truth. Your truth is *what is true for you.*

When friends, family, and society challenge your convictions, it is essential to check in with yourself, to make sure you are still going in the direction you want. One of my favorite quotes of Thoreau's is,

> *If a man does not keep pace with his companions, perhaps it is because he hears a different drummer. Let him step to the music he hears, no matter how measured or far away.*

How do you ensure that you are living at your own pace? No matter how far away the music of your heart is, follow it.

Are you excited to 'check in' with yourself, to see if you're on track?

Secret # 8: Do Your Dailies!
Through Daily Journaling

1. Create your Journaling Ambience ~ set aside at least **10 minutes** for yourself, (no checking email, answering the phone, etc.) Light some candles and incense.

2. To experience the magic of Secret #8, turn on your music player, and play Track 8, *Do Your Dailies SoundTrack,* from the Discover Your Dharma Soundtrack Album.

3. Open to a new page in your journal, and write down the date, time, and your location.

4. Still in the 'writing-super-fast' mode, write chronologically your experiences as they happened from the moment you got up this morning, to the moment you're writing now. Wondering how to capture your daily experience in words? Look at the events that happened today, and then look at your true feelings.

   Example of Secret#8: Do Your Dailies!:

   Let's say the event was: *Went to the dentist.*
   To write the experience, I could write:

   "Today was my last day wearing InvisAlign braces to straighten my teeth. I was so excited to go to the dentist to not wear those painful teeth trays anymore! It is hard to believe that it has already been two years since I first started wearing my braces. I have not only surprised myself with how disciplined and diligent I have been with my orthodontic care, I am also touched by the dedication and support the dentist and his staff have given me. I will miss seeing the staff at my regular appointment every month – to catch up on each other's lives, and their genuine kindness and caring. They have noticed when I got new haircuts, new earrings, or was sick with the flu. They accommodated me when I was late and stuck in traffic, and when I was stressed out about my final exams. It is amazing how strangers who see you for 5 minutes once a

month, can be a part of your life... their kindness and smiles I will always remember..."

5. Write down what was great – all the highlights for today. Celebrate yourself!

   Example: "I don't have a lot of time to go through everything in detail, but I just wanted to write down all the highlights of today for me... what made today awesome? I had the day off from work today – and decided to make the most of it! I did some yoga, meditated, cleaned the kitchen and the living room... and made breakfast with my sister. I struggled a lot today trying to get my work done, and felt like I was getting nowhere. By 4pm, I was a bit frustrated with myself, and watched a couple hours of TV shows with my brother. After dinner – which we ate while watching TV- we finally turned the TV off. The house was quiet, and the only thing I had to do was get my work done. So, I decided to give myself a new deadline – to get everything done by midnight. And for some reason, that was magical. Everything started flowing with ease and grace, and I feel a lot better about myself and my day! Today was a fabulous day! I am making progress, not giving up, and pursuing my dreams! I realize the key to success for me right now is to take one thing at a time, and just go for it!

6. Write down what happened today that you feel troubled over, feel bad about, or made you feel uneasy.

   Example: Today I felt bad about wasting most of my day... I had no excuse and just could not focus and get my work done. Today I said I was going to finish a big project, and I didn't... yet. I feel like I am afraid of finishing, and I make a big deal about this stupid fear, but the reality is, there is no way around it – I just have to jump in and fin-

ish the race. I feel like the future is uncertain, and that I should think about it more, but I do not want to for 2 reasons – 1. Because I have so much to do right now, I don't have time to think about the future, and 2. It really doesn't matter, because when I finish my projects, that will change the picture anyway. The point is... taking right action resolves that bad feeling of wasting time. And that's all there is to it....

7. Take a minute or two to write down a few blessings you are grateful for today. (For more details, see the steps in Secret #10: Gifts of Your Life.)

    Example: Thanks for getting a chance to workout today. Thanks for getting my taxes done. Thanks for clearing my desk. Thanks for having lunch with my friends. Thanks for the fabulous 75 degree weather outside! Thanks for a crazy day today – the fridge was leaking and the electricity went out – thanks that I got help in time, and now everything is fine again. Because of the leak I got to clean the kitchen and mop the floors...Thanks for the chance to get a clean kitchen out of an untimely disaster! It was a good day... thanks for getting my chores done, some progress towards my project, and some time with my friends....

Are you still feeling a little stuck? Here are some of my favorite prompts to make Doing Your Dailies! more fun, insightful, and keep you on track!

What happened in my life today
What was great
What do I want to do
What I don't want to do
What's bothering me
What lessons I have learned today

The blessings of today
Say positive things to myself
Reconnect
Wander
Dream
Goals
Inspiration

Pick any one of the above, and use it as a springboard to reflect on how your day was for you! You will be amazed at how much you have accomplished when you write it down!

8. When you are all done, or when the music is up, SLAM YOUR JOURNAL SHUT, and say out loud, "I DID MY DAILIES!"

When you're done with your Dailies, take a moment to notice how you expressed your self, and if those feelings you expressed were what you really felt inside. We experience many of the same situations on a daily basis, yet often we are a totally different person on the inside than the person we express to the world. We may be screaming or hurting on the inside while we're all smiles and struggling to 'keep it together' on the outside. This is why doing your Dailies is so important.

Keeping track of the outer things is of no importance, if we are not keeping track of our own evolution – what is happening on the inside.

Why do we want to keep track of what is happening, and our feelings? If we are living in the moment, why do we even need to write about our day? And moreover, how does that help with staying on track?

The Power of Daily Journaling

In the traditional art of diary-writing, we either wrote down all the things we did, accomplished, or felt, and that was all. Or we wrote all the qualities we like and don't like, and *that* was all. We rarely ever did both! And the funny thing is neither of them is good without the other! Keeping track of our feelings without taking a look at the whole picture, is of no use if we are not taking a good look at what is triggering those feelings! We may consistently write how upset we feel and walk around like a victim, without once stopping to look at what is triggering it. But put the two together – outer circumstances and inner feelings or responses to those outer things, and you will have a greater success rate at staying on track with your dharma. Why is that?

Daily Journaling helps you to live your dharma by giving you the ability to:

- See how you co-create your life with your Higher Self every step of the way
- See patterns and tendencies that serve you, and those that do not, as you fulfill your dharma
- Witness your dharma unfolding before you, just by looking at the moments of your day, and who you choose to become

As T. Harv Eker says, "How you do anything, is how you do everything." Any one incident you look at is a good indicator of who you are and how you live your life. Remember, all the moments of your day add up to your life purpose!

Through the powerful technique of Daily Journaling, you learn to live more consciously and more authentically. As you practice this effective way of journaling, you exercise the choice to act in alignment with your wisdom from the heart. If you do practice this technique on a regular basis, you will find a new meaning to living consciously: you have to be in the moment so when it is time to write what you ate for breakfast, or what song you heard on the radio that made you smile, you will remember! Soon you will see your life is made up of moments… not days, or weeks, or years.

There is a great power in the celebration of beauty and goodness in your life. Like the quantum observer effect, what you focus on will expand. The more you focus on what you want, the more you will attract it in your life. In the practice of this art, you will begin to see your experiences with a clarity no one can take away. The more you have this clarity, and the more you celebrate yourself, the more you will see the miracles that manifest in your life every day.

Keep on purpose! Keep on keeping on! Hold on to your dreams by the fingernails – the world is good at encroaching upon your time, filling your mind with self-doubt, and demanding your energy elsewhere! Daily Journaling is the tool to cultivate that inner conviction to carry on when confusion creeps in and the luster of our passion begins to fade.

See the miracles and blessings of your day! Embrace the opportunities to expand and to step into something greater than your self. And then anchor yourself in your message, your mission, and your inner power.

If not you,
then who?
Don't dilly-dally.
Do your dailies!

This may be a calendar of the ebbs and flows of the soul; and on these sheets as a beach, the waves may cast up pearls and sea-weed.

Henry David Thoreau, Author, Philosopher, & Journaler

SECRET #9

Stay Connected Within

As optimistic as we are, and as amazing as our dharma is right now, there are going to be times when we are pushed to the limit, and we feel far away from who we want to be. Even though we may know all the answers, we may not always feel connected within. When we feel that our dharma is taking us in directions out of our control, or when we can see our lives changing at lightning speed, that is when we can practice Secret #9. Use it to draw on an inner power from within, a power that will keep you unshaken no matter what happens on the outside.

From Secret #1 to Secret #8, you have taken a closer look at your life, discovered what motivates you, and stepped outside of your comfort zone. You have tapped into what you are passionate about, and you have seen how your passion guides you to your purpose. You have learned the tools to listen to your heart, and how to follow your heart no matter what. In the course of this journey of discovering your dharma, you have seen the big picture, and named it and claimed it for your life.

As you venture forward with a clear vision of your mission, you have the tools to keep on track. Like a pilot flying a plane, you have to use those tools to keep on top of your life, shifting gears through turbulence as you head towards your destination.

There might just be one little problem: what *is* your destination?

According to the Encarta World English Dictionary, the word ***destination*** means:

1. *the place to which somebody or something is going or must go*
2. *a purpose for which somebody or something is intended*

We know all the right things to do, we know all the answers, and yet still, we feel disconnected from our sense of Self, somehow.

Where are you headed? Is it some place on the outside? Or some place deep within Your Self?

Usually, we feel discontented because we are often caught up with trying to fix our outer lives, and we don't get around to looking at our inner lives. When we stop looking at the outside and start developing the ability to look within, we begin to see what is truly real. Our cars, our houses, and our plasma screen TV's, are valuable to us, because we paid for them. But the treasures we have on the inside, we do not put a value on them. We think our inner treasures are valueless when, in fact, they are invaluable. We pay an outside expert for an hour of their time, and that hour has more value than the hour we spend journaling with our Higher Self. Why? Because we value our time with the expert, and not the time we spend with our Selves. When will we choose to see the value of our inner voice - the only one who has the answers for our life?

There is no mirror for us to see how beautiful, wise, and rich we are on the inside, so we think our Inner Self does not exist. Unfortunately, we live in an age where we have to see to believe. If only we could see our Inner Self, we would see how beautiful, wise, and amazing we are! How can we 'see' our Higher Self?

It's time for Secret #9!

Are You Ready?

Secret # 9: Stay Connected Within
Through Spiritual Journaling

1. Create your Journaling Ambience ~ set aside at least **10 minutes** for yourself, (no checking email, answering the phone, etc.,) and light some candles or some incense.
2. Turn on your music player, and play Track 9, *Stay Connected Within Soundtrack,* from Discover Your Dharma Soundtrack Album.

3. Open your journal to a new blank page. Write the date, time, and location.

4. Then, write Dear ______. (In the blank space, fill in whoever you connect with as perfect love, wisdom, and guidance in your life - a Higher Power, Higher Self, Inner Spirit, The Universe, your Guru, a spiritual teacher, Christ, Buddha, family deity, Divine Mother… I think you get the idea, whoever it is for you.)

5. Write down 3 things you are grateful to them for.
   Example:
   Thank you for being with me, for being in my life, and all the blessings you have given me today…

6. Writing with speed and constancy, ask for guidance with things in your life that are complicated and difficult. Ask for guidance in an area of your life where you seem to make no progress, or feel you cannot do anything about.

7. Allow the response of that Higher Power to come to you. Write what flows from your heart through your pen. Feel the ebb and flow of being and conversing with them…talking, listening….listening, talking. Savor the in-between moments as you write; fully partake in the experience of sharing, becoming, enjoying, and being. KEEP WRITING! THAT'S THE SECRET!

8. When the soundtrack is over, or **7 minutes** are up, you can thank your Higher Self for being with you. NOW LOUDLY CLOSE YOUR JOURNAL, and chant the primordial sound of the Universe, "OM."

EXAMPLE of Secret #9: Stay Connected Within

Dear Higher Self,

Thank you for listening to me and for being with me… I have been looking for a job for a month now… and I really need to make some money – fast! I have been doing everything I can to nail a job – meticulously looking on local classifieds, Monster, craigslist.com, and other online job sites. I've been checking these sites morning, noon, and night, and applying for anything I can qualify for. I went back to places I used to work, and talked to people personally to network… I feel soo frustrated! I also gave my resumes to people who can recommend me –parents' friends to refer me to their employers and anyone they know who is hiring. I followed up on referrals and even got a couple offers, but with the economy down, HR depts don't know when the job starts. Tell me who to talk to, tell me what I have to do! Show me where the money is going to come from to pay my bills! What do I do next? Which job fair to go to? I think I did hear of a job fair coming up on campus... I will register for it, revise my resume and prepare for on-the-spot interviews. Thanks! I will also take a temp job while I'm looking for a full-time job... thanks... and yes! I remember my friend Matt said his company is hiring for the summer... I will call him up to see if he can recommend me! These are some better prospects... better face-to-face than blindly sending resumes online... Thanks! OM...

Spiritual Journaling QuickTips

1. Open your journal, and thank your Higher Self
2. Ask for guidance – write any struggles you have
3. Wait for a response, write what comes to you
4. Say 'Om.'
5. Close your eyes for a moment, and sit in the silence of that inner connectedness. Breathe in deeply. And breathe out.

The Power of Spiritual Journaling

By practicing Spiritual Journaling, you will have a direct experience of knowing and connecting with your wisdom within.

Your Higher Self is always there, patiently and eagerly waiting to co-create your life purpose with you! The real secret behind Spiritual Journaling is the first 2 words: Dear ____ (fill in whoever you have a spiritual connection with.) Why are these first 2 words important? They are important in establishing the fact that *your Higher Self/Guru/Inner Spirit is listening to you.* You are writing to them. They are not just anyone who is peaceful and gentle. They are a special being or embodiment of wisdom who completely understands you, blesses you, protects you, unconditionally loves you, and knows you. Whether you remember they are there or not, this Higher Being is with you in your life *always.*

Spiritual Journaling is very powerful as a spiritual practice, or part of a spiritual practice you already have. Some people talk to the Universe all the time. Others can hear the Universe talking to them. Many people pray, sing, or chant to the Universal Spirit, and still others see Him in nature, in their children, or in service to others. Many have written to the Universe asking a question, and the Universe has answered them. But what about simply writing to that Universal Spirit or Higher Self?

Use your pen to talk to the Universe, to your Gurus, to the angels, a spiritual being, your Higher Self, or your own heart's wisdom. Ask questions, and express your feelings, thoughts, fears, hopes, and dreams. Whether you have a spiritual practice or not – it is great to just talk to your higher power – to be loved unconditionally, to have a real relationship and connection with your Self. It is sometimes hard to just pick up a pen and write out of the blues. Why bother writing if no one is listening to us? With this Secret, writing is not the point. It is creating a relationship with your Higher Self, so that someone IS listening! It may seem strange to just pick up your pen and start writing to your Higher Self. Instead, think of this technique as a way of *talking* to your Higher Self through your pen. Let your pen do the talking! Your inner voice will emerge through the words on your paper, and now, you can connect your conscious self with your Super-Conscious Self – through journaling!

Why would you want to have a conversation with your Higher Self? The truth is: it is hard to talk to others about certain personal issues, especially when most people are self-absorbed, judgmental, and rarely understand you well enough to give you great advice. Through this language of journaling, you can build a connection with your Higher Self, and you can receive all the wisdom and inner connection that you seek!

This Ninth Secret is a special element of the entire journey to discover your dharma. All the Secrets up until this point were techniques to get to the heart, to the essence of who you are. In Secrets 1 through 8, you deepened your relationship with yourself, while flushing out of your system, fear, judgment, inner criticism, and guilt. It was like going into an inner sweatlodge - clearing out the toxins, so you can finally see the light. Great job! With some effort and determination, you have used the tools in this course to purify, strengthen, and prepare yourself for this moment – to establish an ever-growing relationship with your Self. Now, you are open, excited, empowered, and ready for the greatness within you to guide your life. It is time to say goodbye to your fears and whiny ego voice. In connecting to your soul, you will find the answers you seek every day; life is ever new, ever changing, and ever evolving, onwards and upwards.

Secret #9 not only makes all of the other Secrets easier to do, but it also gives you an experience of your own Truth on the path of Enlightenment.

These Secrets and Journaling Techniques are the tools to read the compass of your heart, guiding your ship of life over the worldly waters of delusion, into the safe harbor of inner contentment.

If you do not think writing to your Higher Self is real, that is okay. Test it. Do it for even five minutes, and see the magic yourself. Don't have 5 minutes? Practice it when you are sitting at the computer and you want to take a break. Try this technique a few times, and read what you wrote. How do you feel afterwards? What do you notice?

This special technique of Spiritual Journaling is great if you are sad, lonely, impatient, shy, or out-of-sync with yourself. It may be really hard to talk honestly about your personal feelings or personal life to therapists, psychologists, coaches, parents, or friends, for fear of being judged. But try journaling to your Inner Self, a Higher Power, to a wise being, or to the Universe, and you feel a realness, an unconditional love, and an understanding that you cannot yet see in your own self or in those around you. No one can give us this unconditional love, understanding, comfort, compassion, or undying attention we crave, except our own souls anchored in the stillness of inner peace.

The greatest benefit and sole purpose of journaling is to empower you to step into your divinity and embrace your humanity.

What does that mean – to embrace your human-ness, and to step into your Higher Self? While I was writing late into the night, I took a break, and hopped onto the Internet to check my email. I was shocked to see on the news, a picture of firefighters fighting a 30-foot fire in eastern San Diego. My mind was racing… *Oh my gosh – that's today – and that wildfire is twenty minutes from my house!* Heart pounding loudly, I quickly scanned the list of areas that were in danger, and breathed a sigh of relief to see that my city was not on that list. I went to bed, praying for those who might have to evacuate, and hoped that the fire would die down in a few hours. When I woke up the next morning, it looked like sunset; the air was smoky and dense, and the sky was a burnt orange hue. I turned on the television, and was distressed to see that the fire had raged on through the night - burning into nearby towns and spreading north, south, east and west! Ashes flew around like flurries, and covered the grass like snow. Smoke hovered in the streets, and filled the air; it was hard to breathe and our eyes burned from the smoke. Every time the phone rang, we jumped, just in case it was a reverse-911 call ordering us to evacuate. Over the next five days, more than half a million people evacuated their homes. Over 300,000 acres of mountain, groves, businesses, and homes, were all burned to a crisp. More than a thousand families returned to their homes – only to find them completely burned to the ground. From humble cabins in the mountains to lavishly furnished million-dollar homes – all were leveled to ashes. My colleague, Dr. D., was one of those homeowners.

"Dr. D., what are you doing in the lab?" We asked him, shocked that he would come to work a week after the fires.

"I lost my 19 year old son a couple months ago, and now… our home and everything in it is gone to the fires… but you know what? I am still alive. My wife is still alive. Our other kids and grandkids are fine. We have what is most important…*We have each other."*

Tears filled his eyes, as he picked up a family photo that was stuck to a filing cabinet with a magnet. Pointing to the picture, he shook his head, "If we had stayed 15 minutes longer… we would have all been goners. For the grace of God, we heard a fire siren around 3:50 a.m., and we knew – this is it. Now or never! Packed the kids in the car, got the dog, some clothes, and some food… and raced out of Ramona."

It seemed so unreal. One day we were at work, and everything was fine, and the next day, the entire town was burned to the ground. Nothing could ever be the same again.

"Wasn't it hard to go back?" I asked quietly.

To my astonishment, Dr. D smiled, understandingly. "Sure, it was rough going back after a week to see the entire town burned down – the store on the corner, the neighbors, the horse ranch, the electric poles… everything was barbecued! It was like walking into a war zone. Our other car was still in the driveway, but there was no more house! And definitely, I am very sad over losing our home we have lived in for over twenty years. But you know I have never been so happy to hold my family, and to pray with all my heart. I am the luckiest man! *We are still standing – and that is what matters the most."*

I could feel my eyes brimming, fighting to hold back the tears. I looked at Dr. D – his eyes shining and full of life despite the puffy eyelids and dark circles that hung from lack of sleep. Right here, in front of me, stood an ordinary human being who stepped into his own divinity – even if it were only for a moment. Is it really possible - to lose it all, and to still be happy? To have every reason to blame and be angry, and to choose instead, gratitude and joy? To be surrounded with charcoal and ashes, and to still see life as beautiful? Dr. D. is one man among millions of us who have been able to do the same, to see beauty even in the darkest night, to have hope against all odds, and to step into that indomitable power that is our human spirit. A power that is undaunted, unshakable, and unyielding.

Most of the time, we think we are never one of those triumphant, courageous people. They are the Olympians, the heroes, or somebody amazing *out there*. Who are we to embrace our humanity and step into our divinity? Remember Dr. D? There is a divine spark in all of us! Embrace it all! The 'dark' and the Light, the insecurities and the moments of strength – these are all you! Feel that loving Presence ever with you now, especially in times of introspection. Trust in the honest communication you cultivate with your Higher Self, and let go of the burdens of outer existence. Melt into your truth, and the lightness that comes over you as you go deeper into this process. And breathe! Connect to your Higher Self in the quiet peaceful sanctities within you. And realize your essence, your purpose in life: to know You!

If you could only see who you really are!
Beautiful, amazing, powerful, and absolutely Divine!

Character cannot be developed in ease and quiet. Only through experiences of trial and suffering can the soul be 1strengthened, vision cleared, ambition inspired, and success achieved.

Helen Keller, Author & Journaler

SECRET #10

Embrace the Gifts of Your Life

Anne Frank was a truly amazing young girl with so much life and so much wisdom to offer the world. Her diary is an eternal flame to the undying human spirit in all of us.

What strikes me most about Anne Frank is that she wanted to be a famous writer when she 'grew up'. And even though she died in the concentration camp at the age of sixteen, through her spirit and her diary, she *did* fulfill her dharma. Her life, and the way she chose to live it, even in confinement, was captured in her journal. Today, she is a famous author, and an inspiration around the world. Her journal became her legacy. Just as she had intended it to be! Why is her journal so powerful today? It isn't just a recording of the feelings and views of a budding teenager in a dark annex in Amsterdam during World War II. It is her optimism, her authenticity, her willingness to be open to the gifts of life, and her ability to choose love over fear, that makes her immortal.

Can we have that same courage and curiosity about ourselves, and our lives? Can we have the same unwavering faith in the goodness of humanity even when faced with tremendous adversity? Do we have the ability to laugh and to open our hearts to all the blessings in our lives, even if we are in hiding for years, and forced to eat rotten potatoes for months on end?

The key to living your life on purpose is to have gratitude. Not only for the big things or the great things, but also for the small things and the seemingly 'not-so-great' things.

Have gratitude for *everything*.
Why? *Because everything in your life has a purpose.*

Yes, *everything*. Every joy, every sorrow, every kindness, every dark night, every unfulfilled desire, every fleeting moment of victory, everybody, and everything, are in your life for a reason - a very special reason. You may know what that reason is. Or you may not. Why you had to suffer. Why you went the other way. Why things took longer. Why things happened so fast. Why they came. Why they left. Everything occurs for your own soul evolution, for you to fulfill your purpose on this Earth. How blessed you are! Every time your heart is broken, say Thank You! Every time an opportunity comes up, say Thank you! Feel gratitude for the light and the darkness, for without it, you would not be who you are today.

The darkness is not real. It is just there to show you the light. So, see the light! See the doors that open, and the abundance and opportunity that beckon. Look at the words on this page. Aren't they black? Yet, if the words were white, you would not be able to read them, would you? So it is with the struggles in our lives, they are just messages in dark print so it is easier for us to read and understand. That is all. Not to hurt us, but to help us. Not to kill us, but to liberate us from our own delusion.

If you are reading this, and all of this makes no sense whatsoever, then you need to practice this technique of Gratitude Journaling more often in your life. Some people say, "Well, it is not that easy. I am NOT grateful for being poor. I am not grateful that so-and-so hurt me. How can I write that I am grateful? I don't think I could ever forgive them, much more to be thankful!"

Remember the power of words? Energize your words with gratitude, and focus on what you DO have. Be grateful for the money you *do* have. Be grateful that there *are* people who love you. Be thankful for the experience and for the lessons you *will* learn. Just by saying "THANK YOU!" you instantly change the energy and the focus of your consciousness, and you begin to see all the little and big miracles that come to you!

The more you have gratitude, the more blessed you feel, and the more you will see blessings and abundance coming to you in every direction. You may not be able to comprehend how blessed you are or how much there is to be grateful for, until you start doing Gratitude Journaling in your life. Have you ever written down ALL the things for which you are grateful? It will probably take forever, right? That is how powerful the role of gratitude is in your life!

Secret #10: Embrace the Gifts of Your Life
Through Gratitude Journaling

1. Create your journaling ambience ~ set aside at least **10 minutes** for yourself, (no checking email, answering the phone, etc.) Light candles or some incense.

2. Turn on your music player, and play Track 10, *Embrace the Gifts of Your Life SoundTrack,* on the Discover Your Dharma Soundtrack Album.

3. Turn to the next brand new page in your journal. Write the date, time, and your location.

4. In the continuous mode of Stream of Consciousness Journaling, write super duper fast, anything that comes to your head and heart to be grateful for.

   The only rule is: start each sentence with "I'm grateful for...." Or, if you journal to your Higher Self, (or an angel, a spiritual being, or God,) you can start each sentence by saying to Spirit, *"Thanks ______ for..."* and fill in the blank.

   At the Discover Your Dharma Intensive, we will be going into an in-depth celebratory gratitude session exploring your inner truth, fears, experiences or beliefs you are still holding on to. Through the process, you will soak in the blessings of all that you have been through in the past and present, guiding you and celebrating you.

   If you run out of things to write, here are some questions you can start with:
   What are the top 10 things you're most grateful for?
   Who are all the people in your life you're grateful for?
   Who are the people in your life you aren't so grateful for?
   What prayers have been answered recently that you're grateful for?
   What little things happened today that you're grateful for?
   What synchronicities or seeming 'missed opportunities' have happened throughout this dharma journey that you're grateful for?
   What made you smile today that you're grateful for?
   Look around you, within and without, write as fast as you can, all the things you can see and feel, that you're grateful for.

5. When the music is done, or time is up, SLAM YOUR JOURNAL SHUT, and say ALOUD, "THANK YOU!"

6. Breathe in deeply. And breathe out. Feel the peace and quietness of the heart.

Examples:

Here is an example of Gratitude Journaling ripped out of my journal:

January 27, 2009. 9:22 pm Sitting at my desk.

I can't believe it! Thank you for finally finishing my project! Thanks for getting a chance to work on the loose ends last night. Thanks for going to bed at 4 am and for being tired this morning. Thanks for being able to take a nap yesterday. Thanks for helping my friends move to their new apartment. Thanks for everything working out. Thanks for the rain! Thanks for reaching my dentist appointment in time. Thanks for....

Here's an example of Gratitude Journaling in the context of ***Embrace the Gifts of Your Life***:

Today, January 27, 2009, I cannot tell you how much I am grateful for. I am incredibly grateful to be alive right now, to be breathing, to have a human body, to have health in body, mind and soul. To have the freedom to pursue my True Self, and to pursue truth in heart and mind. I am grateful to have all my needs fulfilled, and to be able to laugh, love, learn, give, feel, think, be, and enjoy my relationship with myself, my family, my friends, my colleagues, and all the people in my life. Thank you for the experiences I've had, the places I've lived, the people I've known, the choices I've made, the beauty I've seen, the sounds I've heard, the food I've enjoyed, the moments I've cherished. Thanks for the 'dark' times, the moments I've broken, the nights of despair, the mornings of fear, the times I've been hurt, the people I've hurt....they've all molded me to the person I am today, to have a little more compassion, a little more understanding, a little more angst, a little more kindness.

I am grateful to be on a spiritual path, to be in my family, to have the friends I do have, and to have the depth and love in the relationships I'm in. I am grateful to be the author of this book, to have the ability to share these secrets with others, and in doing so, fulfill my own purpose on this planet. Thanks for the opportunity to be where I am right now, to learn, to grow, to cultivate friendships and relationships with people that I would not have otherwise met. Thank you for the lessons, the struggles, the hard times, the conflict in wanting to know how it all fits, and knowing that I must trust and surrender... and enjoy the journey along the way, becoming more of who I am and expressing that in the world, no matter what I do, or where I go.

Gratitude is the most powerful key to living a life of light, authenticity, integrity, clarity, freedom, forgiveness, and compassion.

Sometimes, we get knocked around by the waves of life, and we do not see that the lesson is right here for us to know. Imagine a little seed pushing against the soil, fighting against the weeds, and hiding from the bugs, struggling to burst above ground just to grow. This is how nature works. We cannot grow unless we have something to push against, to make us stronger, to help us blossom, and to give our gifts to the world. Having gratitude for the hard knocks acknowledges our journey and who we have become as a result of what we had to push against.

I am not saying to keep rolling around in those dark times, dwelling over and over and OVER on what somebody did, or said to hurt you.

My philosophy is: be grateful, forgive, and forget – let go of the pain and the power those painful memories have on your life.

Who wants those unpleasant experiences hanging around? I certainly don't! I know it is really hard to forgive, especially when we do not see the blessing. That is why having gratitude is so powerful – it allows us to heal and it allows us to forgive.

In forgiveness lies our freedom, and our light.

What does it mean to be truly grateful? It is to see that what you are thankful for has had value in your life. But it also means what *will* have value in your life, like being grateful for things you *want*. You might not be living in your dream house right now, but you can still be grateful for your dream house, because there is one out there that is yours, and so, be grateful for it now! Give thanks for 'the good, the bad, and the ugly' because they have all had immense value in your life. Can you imagine your life without any 'bad'? It might be pretty boring and useless, huh? We are always *striving* for a frictionless life, but it is the striving that makes us what we are, not the golden easy life that is not real anyway. Does that make sense? If life isn't a piece of cake most of the time, we might as well be grateful for what we've got! Whatever experiences we have drawn to our lives, are exactly what we needed at the time we needed it. Maybe we needed to learn a very specific lesson, or have an opportunity to fulfill our dharma. Therefore, all of our experiences deserve our gratitude!

Over the past decade of practicing the power of gratitude, I have found that the greatest joys of gratitude come in seeing the miracles of a Higher Power working in my life, taking care of even my littlest of needs. So - give thanks. Especially when the big things come through for you, feel the excitement!

Appreciate all that had to come about to make your dreams come true! Appreciate yourself! Appreciate your accomplishments. Give thanks for anything in your life you can possibly think of. See all your prayers – even unspoken ones – answered in your life, time and time again.

You are amazing, wise, and gorgeous!

I absolutely LOVE Gratitude Journaling and the practice of gratitude in my life. I feel a joyful lightness, like I am floating, when I remember to appreciate people for who they are and what they do for me. In practicing gratitude, I get to have an 'insider's sneak peak' at the Universe's hand behind the blessings. Imagine how great it will be to look back on your day, your year, your life, and see the golden light of gratitude cast on every nook and cranny, every wind and blossom and thorn, filling the skies in golden rays of fulfilled dreams. Our days have many unexpected twists and turns – we run into people, come across an interesting article, hear something inspiring on the radio…and yet still, at the end of the day, we think nothing significant happened, that we weren't blessed at all, and that we didn't do anything grand.

The Power of Gratitude Journaling helps you redefine your day as one more day worth living. Today is one more day you were chosen to be alive, to receive all the blessings, the growth, the joy, the awakening, and the many moments of opportunity to give of yourself, to touch someone else's life, to change the world by who you are, and accomplish what you did today.

Isn't that beautiful?

The Power of Gratitude Journaling

Gratitude is the path to freedom. When we have gratitude, we become free from our fears, judgments, insecurities, emptiness, and feelings of worthlessness. Gratitude attracts abundance; it opens our consciousness to find more things to be grateful for, and therefore create more goodness in our lives. We begin seeing how much our prayers have been answered, and how much we are loved and cared for. In being grateful for even those things that we have to struggle to find gratitude in our hearts, we expand ourselves to see why we attracted this unwanted experience in our lives, and where we still need to grow.

Gratitude is the key to success. Gratitude is the key to enlightenment. Gratitude is the key to truly loving relationships. But, most glorious of all, Gratitude is the key to fully manifesting your Dharma and True Self in this life. Why?

Because, Gratitude is about CELEBRATION!

Be a celebrity in your own life! The more you are grateful, the more you will see things to be grateful for. And the more you are celebrating and loving yourself, the more you will celebrate others, and life. Live a life of celebration! And you will live a life to be celebrated. Imagine what your life would look like if you did that right now.

What are you waiting for?

LET'S CELEBRATE!

And, we'll begin by Celebrating You!

Celebrate your Unique Dharma that only You can fulfill! Celebrate the path you have walked just to be here right now, and celebrate the amazing new Journey you are about to embark on!

Know with certainty that you are not alone – that there are many now and in the future, who will be at your side, supporting and celebrating you!

Open your arms and receive all the blessings being showered upon you at this sacred divine moment.

The time has come.

This IS the hour.

The journey of discovery has unfolded before you, and you have within you all the tools to live your dharma with joy, with intention, with congruency, and with full conviction in Your Truth.

Stand in it.

Walk it.

Be it.

Close your eyes for a moment, and visualize yourself walking on a beach. It is after dusk, and the ocean mist moves onto the beach and the cliffs around you, enveloping you in a cool mystical light. The moon rises slowly, and moonbeams shimmer on the waves as they come and go on the shore. You can hear the light roar of the ocean, the waves lapping against the rocks, and you can see, beyond the mist, the stars brighten, shimmering in the clear skies above. The full moon is now over the hills and is wide and golden. It is a magical night, and you could feel it in the air. You notice along the shore, there is a small bonfire in the distance. As you walk towards it, you can see the outline of a person, adding wood to the fire.

The mist hangs low around you, and in the glowing moonlight, you see the Great Ones appear on the other side of the shore, walking towards you and the bonfire. As you approach the bonfire to-

fire together, they are like old friends, looking into your eyes with warmth and joy. Suddenly, you realize that you are now part of this special band of souls who know the 10 Secrets. One by one, they come forward to hold your hand – Gandhi, Picasso, Da Vinci, Mother Teresa, Disney, Kennedy, Thoreau, Anne Frank, and all the Great Masters and Gurus who have guided you in your soul's journey until this very sacred moment.

As they hold your hand, they put a Lotus Seed of Wisdom in your palm. Each Lotus Seed is the Secret they now give to you - Clarity, Truth, Integrity, Wisdom, Intuition, Vision, Affirmation, Authenticity, Soul Connection, Gratitude, and two more to hold all ten together – Love and Service. These 12 Lotus Seeds of Wisdom are now yours.

Close your hand, and feel the 12 round Lotus Seeds in your palm. Look around you, into the familiar faces by the fire, and feel the warm glowing light illuminate your face while the cool breezes blow calmly about you. As the mist rolls in to surround the warm circle by the fire, you can feel the heat from the flames in your face, and the fire blazing brightly in front of you. The Lotus Seeds have a lightness to them, their grainy luster radiant in the light.

Claim it. Hold it. It is yours.
You have been chosen for a very special dharma.
And that dharma chose you.

The Lotus Seeds of Wisdom have been passed to you.

I honor and celebrate you, as you are honored and celebrated by those who have chosen you, and by the brilliance within you that is represented in those Lotus Seeds you hold in your hand. The luminescence can never go out.

Believe in it.
Believe in yourself.
And remember the sacredness of this moment.

This Moment is Yours.

This is your life, and your destiny lies in who you are this very moment. Feel the excitement and the power surge through Your being!

Open your Eyes:
Before you lies
Your Dharma.

You can do it!

Go for it -

Live Your Dharma!

Ask, and it shall be given you;
seek, and ye shall find;
knock, and it shall be opened unto you:

For every one that asketh receiveth;
and he that seeketh findeth;
and to him that knocketh it shall be opened.

MATTHEW 7:7-8

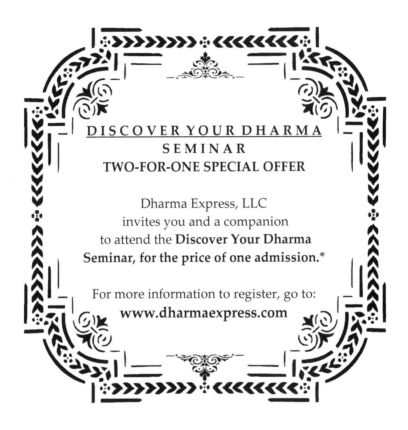

A SPECIAL INVITATION TO DHARMA EXPRESS PROGRAMS & JOURNEYS®

FOR THE DHARMA SEEKERS:

Discover Your Dharma Intensive™ - 2 Days

Come to a place where you can Discover Your Dharma with other Dharma Seekers like yourself. With the excitement and support of dharma seekers from around the world, discover your unique dharma in an empowering experiential power-packed Intensive. This life-changing Seminar focuses on having a personal experience of the tools and benefits outlined in the book, *Discover Your Dharma: 10 Secrets to Redefine Your Life Purpose through Effective Journaling.*

Discover Your Dharma Evening™ and Teleclasses

The Secrets to discover your dharma are taught in evening seminars by Certified Dharma Express® Trainers in select cities around the world. These seminars are also offered as Teleclasses and Webinars online. For details and schedules, see **www.dharmaexpress.com**

How to Live Your Dharma in the Real World – 4 Days

It's one thing to discover your dharma, but a different thing to actually *live* your dharma in the real world every day! Learn the tools to bring your Dharma into action, and live a life of success, purpose, and true fulfillment. In this intensive, you will become your own Visionnaire, and fuel your mission with volition.

Be Fearless and Fight for Your Dharma - 4 Days

At this power-packed program, you will shatter the myths that keep you from steering your course. This program is a must for those who know what their dharma is, but want to have the fearlessness to go out and take right action. Clear the inner path, and follow your heart no matter what!

YOU'VE GOT A BOOK IN YOU™ SERIES:

Discover Your Book Within Funshop™ – 3 Days

Every human being has a story. What's yours? At this Funshop, you will discover your wisdom, your unique perspective, your journey, and your book within! You will also start the process of writing the kernels of your book, and receive coaching while writing your book!

Write-Your-Book Program™ – 4 Days

Designed to empower the modern author who never has time to write, this is a must. At the Write-Your-Book Program, you will learn to conquer writer's block, have the support of the group, and have a structured program for you to explore, write, and edit your work.

Ultimate Write-Your-Book Bootcamp™ – 7 Days

This Bootcamp is a hardcore, high-powered program to get you into gear to finish your book. Under the pressure to write, edit, and complete chapters of your book, you have no excuse but to achieve your goals! Writing coaches and a no-nonsense structure are in place to ensure that you are on track to finishing your book.

DHARMA EXPRESS JOURNEYS™:

Travel to Exotic Countries, and experience heart-opening programs with other like-minded friends!

SPEAKING ENGAGEMENTS

An international award-winning speaker, Shivani Singh is refreshingly fun, highly dynamic, and personally engaging. Her high-energy, life-changing keynote speeches and workshops have inspired countless worldwide to discover their dharma and to express it in the world, through the power of journaling. To have Shivani Singh or one of the Dharma Express speakers speak at your next event, **go to www.dharmaexpress.com for more details.**

Call to Dharma (Right Action!)

Dear Dharma Seeker,

Congratulations! You have just begun to master the secrets to discovering and rediscovering your dharma. Every new moment, your dharma evolves. The word 'dharma' just means, "What is the right action for me to take now?" In the act of asking that question, and doing what we feel is right for us in the moment, we evolve.

The more we live in this conscious way, the more aware we are of who we truly are, why we are here, and what we must do. Who knows? That complete awareness and full realization may come to you in this very instant. Or tonight. Or next year. Or next lifetime. It all depends on you, and your willingness to look inside. Are you brave enough to measure your success by how many times you practiced your soul qualities today? Or are you going to continue to give in to the outer definitions of success, happiness, and other people's expectations?

It's all up to you!

Dan Millman, author of *Way of the Peaceful Warrior,* said, "Knowledge is knowing what to do, and wisdom is doing it." Reading and journaling are powerful – they change your ideas and your consciousness. In the first half of this book, we cleared our minds, recognized our Moments of Truth, Gone Beyond the Line, and Shattered the Myths that keep us from our dharma. These Secrets aren't a one-time deal. Every day, we have new challenges, new questions, and new decisions to make. Do the exercises presented in these Secrets to unlock your truth and your intuition. Every time you have 5 minutes at work on your lunch break, or a quiet moment at the kitchen table on a Saturday morning, practice the Stream of Consciousness, Introspective, or Wacky Crazy Journaling Techniques. I also encourage you to pull out your ***DharmaWheel**** when you feel confused or overwhelmed. Do the declarations at the end of each journaling session so you anchor in your experiences and your wisdom.

In the second half of this book, you learned how to Follow your Heart No Matter What, how to Fuel Your Mission with Volition, how to Be Your Own Visionnaire, and how to Stay Connected Within. You practiced the 5 different Affirmative Journaling processes, and the art of Creative and Daily Journaling. In celebrating and honoring the Gifts of your Life, you've taken a new spin on Gratitude Journaling.

These actions and journaling exercises are vital to being in alignment with your dharma. In changing your consciousness and tapping into your intuition, you will make new choices, new decisions, and thus allow your amazing dharma to unfold! Stimulate those neurons to fire new impulses, new ways of thinking, and new ways of doing things!

We *love* to talk and think and read and pontificate. Rarely do we actually *do* what we know! When that all-too-familiar voice says, "Man, I don't have time for this journaling thing. I'm smart, I'll figure out what to do with my life later…" Be aware of that voice of the ego, the voice of your fears, the voice that keeps you in your uncomfortable little life. Remember that voice is doing its job – to keep you small and safe. Don't give in to it! Journal! Affirm! Celebrate! And take action! It's time to have fun, be happy, and live joyously! Your dharma is unfolding minute after minute – with or without you!

This book, which is like a journal of my own growth and transformation, took me a few years to write. Throughout those

---

* *See www.dharmaexpress.com for your free* ***DharmaWheel***

years, whenever I opened and re-read my work-in-progress, I was always blown away by the wisdom, the answers, and the celebration in these pages; it is amazing to see my own light reflected back to me so clearly! I hope this book does that for you too – not only in sharing with you these secrets, and encouraging you to transform your own perspectives, but to find a light within these pages that will inspire you to step into your own greatness. I hope you turn to this book to be reminded that you have all the answers within - even when you're down on life, even when you're stuck and overwhelmed, or even when you feel you have no clue where your life is going. At those times, (which happen more often than we care to admit,) read a chapter or two, and take 5 minutes to journal. This practice will help you bring yourself back into alignment, to reconnect with who you are – your beauty, your vibrance, your vision, and your wisdom.

Visit www.dharmaexpress.com and click on "DHARMA FREEBIES" to receive more cool gifts to help you stay on track with your dharma. The freebies include:

- The DailyDharma Thought of the Day
- The Discover Your Dharma 'action kit'
- The Discover Your Dharma 'journal starters'
- A Complimentary ***DharmaWheel***

While I do believe that there is a special magic to practicing these secrets on your own, I have personally witnessed thousands of breakthroughs and transformation for people all over the world in our group programs. The friendship, support, and power of the group energy focused on pursuing their dharma no matter what, is truly an extraordinary experience. With my sincerest love and friendship, I invite you to attend the **Discover Your Dharma Intensive Program**. This event will take you to a completely new level of alignment with your Dharma.

One of my favorite quotes by Howard Thurman is:

Don't ask what the world needs. Ask what makes you come alive, and go do it. Because what the world needs is people who have come alive.

What makes you come alive? When are you going to do it? It is my mission to do what makes me come alive, and the more I passionately help others to discover and live their dharma, the more this world will be full of truly happy, purposeful, and abundantly joyous people!

It is my heartfelt hope that through the life-changing processes shared in our books and programs, you realize that within you is all that you seek, and that you have the tools to Discover and Live your DHARMA TO THE FULLEST!

To all the happiness that is yours in living your dharma!

With all my love,
Shivani